YORKSHIRE

of one hundred years ago

The Windmill at Hessle

YORKSHIRE

of one hundred years ago

DAVID GERRARD

SUTTON PUBLISHING

First published in 1997 by
Sutton Publishing Limited · Phoenix Mill
Thrupp · Stroud · Gloucestershire · GL5 2BU

British Library Cataloguing in Publication Data
A catalogue record for this book is available from the British Library

ISBN 0 7509 1422 X

Half-title photograph: Yachting at Bridlington
Title page photograph: Street violinist, Hull
Front endpaper: Hope Bank United Sing, 1907
Back endpaper: Group near The Cod and Lobster, Staithes

 ALAN SUTTON™ and SUTTON™ are the trade
marks of Sutton Publishing Limited

Typeset in 11/13pt Bembo Mono.
Typesetting and origination by Sutton Publishing Limited.
Printed in Great Britain by WBC, Bridgend.

In the sizing warp threads room, Kaye & Stewart's Broadfield Mills, Lockwood, Huddersfield

CONTENTS

The passenger ship Humber *at Spurn Head*

PREFACE

In Roy Hattersley's words, 'Yorkshire is not just a place, but a state of mind'. This anthology seeks to portray both the place and the state of mind as it was about one hundred years ago.

All but a very few of the photographs were taken between 1880 and 1914. During this period a minor social revolution was effected by the GPO's decision in 1894 to accept picture postcards for delivery. (The stamp cost a halfpenny and for several years the reverse of the card could only be used to write the address.)

Picture postcards were a spectacular success and, as a result, almost every church, chapel and market cross, the most obscure hamlets and the most nondescript views were systematically photographed. The vast majority of these cards are now of only local interest since many commercial photographers deliberately excluded people. Fortunately, there were also many more adventurous photographers and it is their pictures which are included in this book, along with the work of gifted amateur photographers and professionals like the incomparable Frank Meadow Sutcliffe of Whitby whose studies of the people and places of the North Riding are both technically impeccable and artistically inspired.

The text extracts printed here were also either written between 1880 and 1914, or record the authors' recollections of that time. I can't prove this statistically, but it seems to me that more books were written in the late nineteenth century about Yorkshire than about any other part of England. Many of them are stultifying – banal reworkings of the same historical anecdotes and moribund legends. But there were also authors like the urbane general practitioner Dr R.W.S.

Bishop whose book, *My Moorland Patients*, is hugely entertaining; the country town solicitor, C.J.F. Atkinson, privy to some discreditable secrets of his farmer clients; and the socialist councillor Ben Turner who, with the characteristic bluntness of the 'tyke', titled his autobiography *About Myself*. I have also included several selections from less orthodox sources (such as the *Huddersfield College Magazine*'s account of a disastrous Sports Day in 1891, for example) where these throw light on matters usually ignored in the conventional literature.

Attempting to provide a faithful mirror of the active, various and complex society that flourished in the Yorkshire of 100 years ago has been a fascinating undertaking and the completion of this volume would have been impossible without the generous assistance I have received from many people across the county. Detailed acknowledgements appear on p. 113, but I would particularly like to thank Mrs J. Pickup of Pickering who allowed me free access to her late husband's remarkable collection of old photographs of the North Riding, and Ken Jackson of 'Memory Lane' in Hull whose treasury of more than 10,000 pictures of the East Riding has yielded some of the most striking images in this book. Special thanks are also due to Mr M.Y. Ashcroft, North Yorkshire County Archivist; Mrs Ellen Law of The Swaledale Museum, Reeth; Mrs A.E. Matthews, Hampsthwaite; Ray Wilkinson at the Stable Lads Welfare Association, Middleham: and to the unfailingly helpful staff at libraries across the county: Elizabeth Melrose (Northallerton); Jane Helliwell (Huddersfield); Sandra Smith (Leeds); Alex Bromley (Hull) and Carol Greenwood (Bradford).

The North Beach at Scarborough, c. 1895

INTRODUCTION

One hundred years ago, Yorkshire – along with the rest of the British Empire – was preparing to celebrate Queen Victoria's Diamond Jubilee. In Huddersfield the Town Council formed a special 'Committee for Local Rejoicings' to commemorate her 'Sixty Glorious Years'. So special was this event that even the austere régime of the workhouses was temporarily relaxed. The Guardians of the Pickering Workhouse, for example, authorised the payment of 6d (2½p) to each child in their care and ordered that each inmate should be served 'a special tea with double allowance of Bread, Tea, Sugar and Milk, to finish off with one buttered hot cake each'.

These were bright confident days for the British. Their Queen and Empress headed the most extensive Empire ever known, and a seemingly invincible Navy sustained Britain's rôle as the only truly global power of the time. In the great manufacturing cities of the West Riding, monumental Town Halls and other public buildings symbolised the overweening self-confidence of the age and, even in the nursery, infants absorbed the imperial ethic along with their ABC:

> C is for Colonies
> Rightly we boast
> That of all the great nations
> Great Britain has most.

The pomp and panoply of the Jubilee celebrations cast a gorgeous cloak over the true state of the nation. For most of the quarter-century before 1897, Yorkshire's industrial centres had suffered the chill of a world-wide recession. As recently as 1880, Britain had been the paramount trading nation with 25 per cent of world trade in its hands: by 1910 that share would drop to 15 per cent, overtaken by the United States and Germany. But in this Jubilee Year the smoke belching from the chimneys of the West Riding mills showed no sign of abating. The boom town of Middlesbrough, a barely visible hamlet of four houses and twenty-five residents in 1801, had just seen its population pass the 100,000 mark. And on Humberside, the tonnage passing through the port of Hull was exceeded only in London and Liverpool. These glowing examples of Capitalism Triumphant masked the beginnings of a leisurely decline that would continue through most of the twentieth century.

The plight of agricultural communities across the three Ridings, on the other hand, was more evident. Land values had fallen dramatically since the early 1880s and, to make matters worse, the county had suffered a series of meteorological disasters. Almost continual rain fell throughout the summer of 1879, destroying nearly 80 per cent of crops and causing millions of sheep to die from sheeprot. A series of bad harvests followed and then the winter of 1885–6 brought the heaviest

Kirkbymoorside Brass Band at Castle Howard, 1897

King Edward VII at Londesborough Park,
c. 1904

snowfall for more than a century, the snow lying so deep that it obliterated drystone walls and entombed whole flocks of sheep. Farmhouses in the Dales were cut off for several weeks.

With hindsight we can see that the Jubilee celebrations took place not on the flood tide of imperial glory but in its waning ebb. And for millions of those taking part in the festivities, their citizenship of what was still the world's most prosperous society brought meagre material rewards. Just 3 per cent of Britons owned 30 per cent of the nation's wealth, a further 9 per cent (described as 'comfortable') held on to a further 14 per cent while the remaining 88 per cent of the population ended up with an average annual income of £23.

The consequences of this grossly unequal distribution of wealth were painstakingly recorded by Seebohm Rowntree whose Quaker family had founded the chocolate firm in York in 1869. In *Poverty: A Study of Town Life*, published in 1901, he lists in minute detail the budgets, spending habits and living conditions of working-class people in his home city. A typical entry describes a married couple, both aged 25, with three children under four years old, subsisting on a disposable income of 2*s* 6*d* a week: ' . . . the children look ill and rickety, and are very small and poorly developed, . . . eat little at meal times, but have sweet biscuits given them between meals. . . . The family is heavily in debt. The protein in this family's diet only amounts to one-half of the standard requirements.'

Rowntree also examined the medical records of 3,600 Army recruits who applied for enlistment at York, Leeds and Sheffield between 1897 and 1901. The examiners rejected 950 (26½ per cent) of them because of their physical unfitness. A further 760 (21 per cent) were accepted provisionally to see if a few months of Army food and training would bring them up to standard: a standard, incidentally, that had been

Celebrating the Relief of Mafeking, 23 May 1905

Gypsy encampment at Boroughbridge for the Horse Fair

repeatedly revised downwards so that by 1901 the minimum requirements for an infantry soldier were a height of 5 ft 3 in, a chest measurement of 33 in and a weight of 8 st 3 lb.

Malnourishment was endemic in the serried back-to-back terraces running up the flanks of the Pennines and in the colliery villages of the South Yorkshire coalfield, but on the farms it was a different story. Farm labourers were poorly paid – the average wage was around 8*s* a week – but as C.J.F. Atkinson put it: 'In the substantial farm houses, eating and drinking were held in great respect. People could neither work nor play if they were poor eaters.' Three hearty meals a day were supplemented by tea at four o'clock and generous quantities of home-brewed ale. It was a matter of both pride and self-interest for a farmer to provide a groaning table for his workers – self-interest because word quickly spread and at the Michaelmas hiring fairs he would have the pick of labourers looking for a change of employer.

The Hiring Fair, at which workmen and women arrived bearing their badge of employment (a crook for a shepherd, a mop for the maid), was a fixed point in the rural calendar. Business done, the day was given over to various sports and such 'highly diverting items' as the pipe-smoking competition. Men sat on a wall and were given a clay pipe filled with cut-up twist tobacco. 'At a given signal they all lit up and the prize went to the one who could make the tobacco last the longest without letting it go out. The facial expressions of the competitors as they tried to draw life into a dead wad of tobacco would bring shrieks of delight from the spectators.'

Fairs like these, Wakes Days, village Feast Days and Market Days all provided relief from the gruelling toil of farm or factory but what was most appreciated was a really good funeral. The family breadwinner might scrimp on other necessities but was scrupulous in paying his few pence a week into a Burial Fund to provide fitting hospitality for the guests at his funeral. 'The more heavy the feast, the more honour done to the dead' observed Miss M.W.E. Fowler. 'Ham is a great feature on these occasions, "to be buried wi' 'am" being very correct'.

Working-class weddings, by contrast, were comparatively plain affairs. Lady Bell, whose husband owned several Middlesbrough steel mills, took an active interest in the lives of her husband's employees. Among the many interesting observations in her book *At the Works*, she describes how casually the young mill-workers committed themselves to marriage. The ceremony itself would be attended only by the couple and two witnesses. 'After the wedding is over they go back to their own house, and either have a day off and enjoy themselves, or else the man goes straight back to work and the wife to her new home.'

Lady Bell's comments form one of the 150 extracts in this book. They have been grouped into eight main sections covering such themes as the Yorkshire character, Victorian childhoods, sport and leisure, work and so on. Together with the many photographs, I hope they will provide an insight into a society so different in many ways from our own, although it came to an end only just beyond living memory.

David Gerrard
Constable Burton
North Yorkshire

'A MOST INTERESTING PEOPLE'

W hile the Scots ('stingy'), the Welsh ('garrulous') and the Irish ('slow-witted') have had those stereotypes thrust upon them by other nations, it was Yorkshire people themselves who were the most enthusiastic creators of their own type-casting. Almost every book written about the county around the turn of the century contained a lengthy analysis of the Yorkshire character. The typical Yorkshireman, they concurred, was hospitable and kindly, forthright, with a shrewd wit and a canny head for business.

However, these admirable traits were often seen by less partisan (i.e. non-Yorkshire) authors as unappealing vices. 'Honesty and directness' in one writer's book becomes 'appalling rudeness' in another's; thrift shades into miserliness; pride in their county degenerates into insularity and an 'utter contempt for Southerners'.

Even Yorkshire writers had little time for the 'tyke' – a West Riding type who displayed an 'utter disregard for anybody's feelings' and whose 'one standard of value is money'. The normally sympathetic country solicitor, C.J.F. Atkinson, whose unflattering portrait of the tyke is included in this chapter, ends his character assassination with the words '. . . they give dear old Yorkshire a bad name. That is why I have not spared them.'

Countless anecdotes were told to illustrate the Yorkshire character. In Across the Broad Acres, the Revd A.N. Cooper tells of a man he knew who owned a small piece of land in the middle of a great landlord's estate. 'The big man wanted to get it at any price, and offered to cover it with sovereigns. To this the owner agreed, but when the agents came, prepared to fulfil the bargain, and laid the money flat on the floor, the owner said, "Nay! I meant the sovereigns to be placed edgeways!"'

In the same book, the Revd Cooper recounts the story of a Yorkshireman arriving at a remote inn one wet night to find every bed taken. A stranger, pitying his plight, offered to share his bed. At bed time 'the owner of the room politely asked the Yorkshireman if he preferred to lie on the right or on the left side. To this came the startling rejoinder: "You can lie which side you like but I intend to lie in the middle!"'

It was a Scottish couple, Thomas and Katherine McQuaid, who after travelling extensively through the three Ridings during 1894, delivered perhaps the simplest and most succinct estimate of the Yorkshire character: 'The people are', they declared, 'most interesting'.

In a Bradford park

CARRYING SELF-RESPECT BEYOND A VIRTUE

The people are most interesting; they are almost always kind and genial, full of a quaint racy humour, and, spite of their proverbial thrift, hospitable to strangers. The dialect differs in the three Ridings; it is not easy to understand, but even when unintelligible there is in it a quaint mellowness of sound in perfect keeping with the comfortable well-kept cottages, nestling two and three together under a tree, or with the large gray farmsteads, surrounded by golden ricks, of which we got glimpses in our journeys through the broad dales that are such distinctive features of the county.

We visited many of the cottages, and were invariably surprised by the exquisite cleanliness of even the poorest; the walls and rafters looked as if they had been newly white-washed, while the metal knobs of the stove glistened with brightness; every article of furniture looked as if it had never known a speck of dust, and the door-stone and lintel were usually a bright fresh yellow. In Wensleydale we saw a pattern chalked on the door-steps and all round the edge of the living-room floors. The people seem to have an utter contempt for Southerners not only with respect to their powers of house-cleaning, but for their general capacity; indeed it may be said of Yorkshire folk that in all ways they carry self-respect beyond a virtue. They seem to be a practical, sensible, but unimaginative race, and are therefore more likely to make money, and to keep it when made, than to understand or do justice to qualities which they do not possess.

Thomas and Katherine McQuaid

AN EXTREME EXAMPLE OF THRIFT

The following is an extreme example of thrift and greediness. The vicar of one moorland parish, who had a fancy for rare breeds of poultry, one day unexpectedly purchased a pen of birds of quite a new variety, but had no run ready for them. He approached a neighbouring farmer who had an isolated farm building, asking him to take charge of them for a few weeks till accommodation was ready, and to keep the eggs in return for the keep. As they were all laying, it was a profitable bargain for the farmer, and he readily consented. A few days afterwards the vicar went for a sitting of eggs, and, knowing his man, offered him the market price of a shilling per sitting. 'Nay, Nay, Nay,' said the farmer. 'Them's a particular soart, and Ah's sellin' 'em at two-and-sixpence a sitting,' and he declined to let the vicar have the sitting at a lower rate.

R.W.S. Bishop

Market Day, High Street, Wetherby, c. 1910

The Shepherds' Retreat Club, Lealholm

SAVINGS IN AN OLD STOCKING

We smile at the idea of savings being deposited in the old stocking or the secret chimney-corner, but it is not long ago, speaking in this enlightened year of 1898, that after our Actuary had emphasised the danger of keeping money with such inadequate protection in a cottage, a sum of £30 – stocking and all – was brought for deposit in the Yorkshire Penny Bank.

Again, it is only a short time since that an elderly gentleman came and solicited an interview with one of the principals. After discussing the investments of the Bank, the Reserve Fund, the Rules, &c., for a quarter of an hour, during which time we had formed the opinion that it was his purpose to deposit the savings of a life-time, he informed us that he was perfectly satisfied and would open an account in which he deposited 2s 6d [12½p].

One more example I should like to quote of a peculiar character. A few days ago, a depositor, a hard-working and respectable man, gave notice that he wished to withdraw the amount of his account, viz: £300. To him it was all he had, and it was quite right that he should look after it, but his methods were curious. The money was duly paid over to him, but after carefully counting and handling it, he returned it with the remark that it was all right, he only wanted to see it.

H.B. Sellers

A souvenir photograph for the Coronation, 1911

The Bishop of Sheffield (left) and Archdeacon Sandford, c. 1901

WHY YORKSHIREMEN SPEAK THE TRUTH

The Bishop of Bradford some time ago referred to the forthrightness of Yorkshire folk. 'The difference' (he said) 'between an Irishman, a Welshman, and a Yorkshireman is that the Irishman does not speak the truth because he thought what he said would please you more. The Welshman does not speak the truth because he does not know the difference between the truth and the other thing . . . but the Yorkshireman speaks the truth because he does not care a hang for anyone on earth.'

J. Fairfax-Blakeborough

SCORN FOR A 'SOCIETY HUMORIST'

I remember on one occasion, when being driven to the station by a real old Yorkshire coachman – I had been one of a house party for three days as society humorist – the old fellow giving me a huge dig with his elbows, and saying, 'Ah saay, is yon all you deea fer a living?' 'That is all,' I replied. 'Well, by goa! bud ya git yer living easy, you deea.' 'I don't know; if you had all the knocking about that I have perhaps you would not think it quite so easy,' said I. 'Whya, Ah deean't know; what ya'll 'ev yer expenses paid, 'even't ya?' 'Certainly,' I answered. 'Aye; an' ya git fed fer nowt, deean't ya?' 'Of course,' I replied, greatly amused. 'Whya then,' said he, 'Ah'll tell ya what: ya travel fer nowt, yer sheltered fer nowt, fed fer nowt, an' ya deea nowt; Ah leeak upon ya ez nowt i' t' wo'lld else bud a aristocratic pauper.' 'Wait a moment,' said I; 'don't you think brains count for something in a matter of this kind?' And then, with that ineffable scorn which I think only the Yorkshireman of that type can assume, he said, 'Braans! braans!! braans!!! Ugh, Ah've ez monny brains ez you 'ev if they war nobbut scraped oot.'

Richard Blakeborough

A JUDGE WITH LITTLE 'HOSS SENSE'

His Honour Judge —— for some little time had a house in a Cleveland village, and whilst there he did a bit of 'hoss swapping' with one of the farmers. Unfortunately his Honour's horse did not turn out well. Meeting the farmer one day, he said, 'Robert, you took me in with that horse, it has turned out very badly.' 'Hez 't, noo? Whya, that'a a bad job; bud you maun't gan blethering aboot 'at Ah've ta'en ya in, or else fau'k'll get it 'i ther heeads 'at ya're nobbut a varra poor judge.'

Richard Blakeborough

AN ECCENTRIC SPORT

I hardly know any Yorkshireman who does not fancy a bit of sport. It is sometimes carried to eccentric lengths. I once heard of the owner of a Yorkshire mansion whose kitchen was infested with rats. Most of us, if we thought we had a rat on the premises, would conceal it from our neighbours like a thing of shame, and do everything to expel the menace. Not so our Yorkshire sportsman. When we had a dinner party he loved to say after the meal, 'Let's hunt rats,' and lead the company into the kitchen, where, with many barbaric cries, they poked rats off the shelves for the terriers waiting below.

We have read of another host, no less eccentric, who for a joke used to have dinner served in reverse when he had new and shy guests. After fortifying appetite with coffee and a cigar, followed by a glass of port, they would have cheese and then a sweet, and so on, back to soup and sherry, and, finally, cocktails. The simple host considered it a great comic achievement if all his guests backed through the menu thus without comment or question.

William Linton Andrews

Hovis and Turog bread delivered to your door

Appleton Hall, near Northallerton

A 'RIGHT DO' WITH THE ORDNANCE SURVEY

A sturdy yeoman met me on a walk one spring day, and asked, 'What's this 'ere ordnance survey they're going into all our land for?' When I had explained, he went on, 'Well, I had a right do wi' one o' them surveyor chaps yesterday. I found him wi' his instruments and things in the middle of my best meadow field, walking about and treading all t' grass down. I says to him, 'Now, young man, come out o' that close.' He looked at me if I wor nowt, and said, 'I shall do nothing of the kind. I am taking the ordnance survey.' I says, 'Ye'll tak' nowt out o' there. I pay rent for that meadow, and if there's owt to be ta'en I'm going to tak' it misen.' 'But,' he says, 'I'm making a survey.' So I says, 'Then mak' it on t' road, and don't tread my grass down.' He says, 'But I'll show you my Government instructions,' and he pulls about half a yard o' paper out, 'Look at that,' he says. I says, 'I s'all look at nowt, but thee look at my grass, thou's stamping it all to muck. Now,' I says, 'is ta coming out quietly, or hev I to force thee out?' So he says, 'No. I'm going to finish my work.' 'We'll see,' I says. So I went into t' farm buildings and I lowses out a young bull 'at hed been teed up t' winter, and I leads him down t' lane, and turns him into t' meadow. T' bull took two or three mouthfuls o' grass, and then he looks up at t' surveyor chap, puts his head down and his tail up, gives a gurt bawl and runs at him. T' surveyor seed him coming and shouts out, 'Here, call that beast off. What do you mean?' I says, 'Let t' bull lewk at the Government instructions, lad!' But he didn't stop. He wor quick ower t' fence and t' bull went racing round t' meadow with his instrument things on his horns till they dropped off, an' I picked 'em up an' threw 'em ower t' fence. Then t' surveyor began to be civil and after a bit o' fair talk, I helped him wi' his measuring, and got him away. I'd ha' done that from t' start if he'd nobbut been civil.'

C.J.F. Atkinson

THE SOUR SIN OF AVARICE

John and William were twins. They may have been alike when they were born, but no two brothers in this world were so different in temperament. Their character showed itself in their faces and bearing as they grew up. John had an open sunny face, clear honest eyes, and an upright sprightly form. William had a creepy, stooping figure, and always looked as if he was trying to slink out of sight, as he might meet someone who would want to punish him. His eyes were little and shifty, his lips thin and hard, his jaw coarse and heavy. You would have trusted John by his looks, just as you would have distrusted William by his. Even William's smile was sinister – he just squeezed up his queer little eyes and dropped his jaw at you. When he spoke he lowered his voice to a whisper, and came close to your ear, as if he was ashamed of being heard. If he returned the usual greeting of 'Good morning. Fine day,' he did it with a husky note of interrogation, as if he was afraid of being asked to guarantee something.

John in early manhood fell in love with a pretty young school teacher who came to the village. The marriage was a very happy one, and they had five bright little children. William remained a bachelor. He had once courted the daughter of an aged and rather miserly farmer, who was reported to be rich, but after her father died, he went to Wakefield, paid a shilling at the Probate Registry, saw the will and got to know how much the estate was sworn at. He was surprised to see the figure so low – as a matter of fact the old man was possessed of a good deal of copyhold land in the Forest of Knaresborough – an old tenure which was not then included in executors' probate accounts. So William jilted the girl, and got a sour-faced housekeeper to do for him at his farm. She suited his habits because she was strictly economical. The neighbours said 'she would skin a flea for its hide and tallow,' or 'would split a currant in two.'

On one occasion, and one only, had William been known to offer to stand a drink in the market town. At the big farmers' 'Ordinary' dinner in the King's Arms, he happened to sit next the new Vicar, who had just come to the village, and was down in the town on business. Thinking that friendliness might be profitable, he said, 'Will you have a glass of beer with me, Vicar?' The clergyman said, 'Thank you' and took it. When William went home, he said to his housekeeper, 'I allus thowt all parsons wor teetotal, or I wodn't ha' spokken.' He always 'got fresh' at the rent day dinner – because the landlord was paying the bill.

C.J.F. Atkinson

Five 'bright little children' of the Revell family, Rosedale

FEELING 'LIGHTSOMER' TODAY

The very words in that wondrous Yorkshire speech have a virtue of their own. When you say that a man is very 'oppositious,' you use a word which you will not find in the dictionary, and, what is more, you will hardly find as pregnant a word there for that which it denotes. A young barrister, who prided himself on the purity of his English, betrayed his origin by saying of one of two paths which presented themselves in the course of a walk, 'This is the gainest way.' Can any word express the real advantages of a path so well as that 'gainest?' You visit an ailing man, and ask him how he is, and he says he feels 'lightsomer' today. Do we not almost feel that we share the sense of relief from the burden and depression of sickness as we listen to the music of that word? On the other hand how much is meant by 'middlin'' when it has its qualifying word attached to it, and its appropriate tone! 'I'm middlin' like' means that a man is exceedingly well, but that it would be tempting Providence to say so, and that it is far better to understate the condition of one's health than to express it superlatively. On the other hand when one says, 'I'm nobbut middlin',' there is a brave repression of the true state of the case. The man feels bad, but he will not so belittle himself as to say so, but will give you a window through which you may see his state, and may render him your sympathy.

A distinguishing characteristic of this racy Yorkshire speech, and one which may cause difficulty, is its terseness. It is generally believed that the Yorkshireman has an infinite power of talk, and I am not denying that this is often the case. But it is also necessary to affirm that no one can exceed the Yorkshireman in economy of speech, when he is so minded.

No better example of this, or of the dry humour underlying it, can be given than that which Viscount Cowdray has related. He says that his father-in-law had a market room near the Bradford Exchange. As he sat there on market days, a certain spinner would poke his head round the door and the following conversation would often ensue:

SPINNER. Mornin', Sir John. Owt?
SIR JOHN. Not to-day.
SPINNER. Nowt! Mornin'.

William E. Anderton

'US CHAPS WOD DEW OWT SOONER NOR WRITE'

The practice of a country solicitor gives great opportunities for the study of human nature. The relationship between a lawyer and his clients is much more personal in the country than it is in city offices. He knows a great deal more, not only about their property, but their family affairs, and sometimes even their horses and cattle. In my early days, it was quite common for a lawyer to leave his office from about 11 to 12 on a market day, and stroll about the little town, chatting with everyone he met, and looking out for people whom he wished to see.

The Hattersley narrows machine at Kaye & Stewart's Broadfield Mills, Lockwood, Huddersfield

The Market Place, Beverley

'Has So-and-so come down to the market today?' he might say, and the answer might be, 'Yes, I have not seen him, but I know he's here, because I saw his dog feightin' in t' Black Bull Yard.'

This often saved a great deal of time, because farmers were, in those days, not accustomed to letters, and they did not like the strain of answering them. 'Ye knaw, us chaps wod dew owt sooner nor write.' They did not answer letters, they let them wait 'until they chanced to leet on you,' and then they would reply by word of mouth.

C.J.F. Atkinson

THE YORKSHIRE 'TYKE'

In most of my character sketches, I have been describing the country Yorkshireman, with his kindly, shrewd humour and candour. I am now turning to a different class – a certain type occasionally found in the West Riding towns, whom for want of a better word I will call 'the tyke.' He is very different from the dalesman, for he has very little imagination, no power to put himself in another man's place,

Captain F. Chapman

and little capacity to see any way but his own. His one standard of value is money, and his thick neck, heavy jaw, small inquisitive eyes, and utter disregard for anybody's feelings, usually mark him as a man who has made a good deal of money. But he is often so hard a bargainer that he defeats his own ends. Everyone is ready for him. For want of imagination he misses good chances. He will never accept an offer without trying to qualify it, and so he often spoils a deal. He puts himself wrong by trying for too much, excusing himself on the plea that 'there is no harm in asking.' Of course, there is a great deal of harm in asking for that which will make the other man think you take him for a fool. He is hopeless at any kind of debate. If his opponent sets a trap for him, he will walk straight into it, simply because his eyes of imagination are too darkened to see it. He can nearly always be 'drawn' to interrupt just where a smarter opponent wants it. He will never be restrained from saying anything because it is 'not good form.' If he wants to know a gentleman's income or a lady's age, he will just ask them, even in the presence of strangers. He often 'gets on' financially because of this complete lack of sensitiveness. When others hesitate, he goes for his object 'through muck or nettles.' He is never silent from fear of making a fool of himself. He is too self-centred to see that he can make anything of the kind.

Perhaps the worst of this type is that he thinks it weakness to be polite. But if he is paid back in the satire which he deserves, he is the touchiest of men to take offence. He will not reason, because he cannot. Any argument makes him lose his temper. One of his special characteristics is a rooted prejudice against educated men. He has no use for education unless it 'makes brass.' A man who speaks good clear English, and not his own uncouth accent, irritates him.

I wish to repeat that men of this type are exceptional, but they exist, and they give dear old Yorkshire a bad name. That is why I have not spared them.

C.J.F. Atkinson

WIT OF THE TYKE

A story is told of an old character in Wensleydale, who had all the straightforwardness and wit of the tyke. On one occasion the then Master and a solicitor were riding along to the hunt fixture when they fell in with old A——.

Said the Master, 'Will there be a scent, this morning, A——?'

The old man, who was steeped in the lore and laws of venery, answered, 'Nut wahl t' sun's on t' wane; then there will.'

'Thanks!' was the reply.

A—— stood for a moment, and then said, 'If you'd assed him 'ats wi' ye, he'd a charged ye six an' eight-pence; but ah nivver charges na mair an' a bob mesell.'

Needless to say he got his 'bob.'

Captain F. Chapman

AN 'ODOUR OF MAN' ABOUT THE HOUSE

If measured by years, rather than by the change the years have wrought, no long time has passed since a certain maiden lady lived here – a maiden lady whose memory still brings the scent of rose-leaves with it. She lived within a stone's-throw of those rollicking, rough-handed wool-combers who made Bingley a pitfall to the stranger; but the outer life passed by her, while she tended her flowers, and made her wines – of elderberries, and currants black and red – and moved, with quiet and unsuspecting dignity, toward the grave that could scarce be more peaceful than the gentle order of her days had been.

This old maid did not merely dislike men; she had a horror of them – the instinctive shrinking that some people have from cats. If a carpenter had to be called in, she would open doors and windows wide after he had gone, and 'Mary,' she would say to her favourite servant, 'there is *an odour of man* about the house. We must keep the windows open, Mary, until the rooms are sweet again.' Her tenants came twice a year to pay their rents; and on these occasions the mistress of the house, moved by a self-sacrificing sense of hospitality, invited them to enter the forbidden precincts. Chairs were set in a formal line round the kitchen, and upon these the tenants sat for a chilly quarter of an hour, while they drank a glass of home-made wine, and ate their sponge-cake, and watched the little lady flutter disturbedly about the open door, as if fresh air were needful to her during the ordeal. Then, after they had finished their cakes and wine, their hostess would take a cambric handkerchief, place it in her tiny, well-bred palm, and hold it out for the reception of the moneys; and after that her tenants would bow themselves through the creeper-covered door and down the well-kept drive.

Not on any account would the old lady touch men's hands, or money that had been in them; when she went into the street she wore gloves that were an inch or so too long, and any gentleman who knew her ways – and who did not in Bingley? – understood that etiquette forbade him to do more in the way of greeting than shake the limp glove-fingers. They remember yet how a new vicar came to the village who was ignorant of these characteristics, and they describe how the parson and his sensitive parishioner met for the first time in the street. The vicar wished to be cordial with an important and pleasant member of his flock; he shook her warmly by the hand, not by the glove-fingers; he approached her more nearly than any gentleman of the neighbourhood had dared to do this score years past. And the little lady, they say, went whiter and whiter, despair warring with politeness; for every forward step of the vicar's

Bingley Wesleyan Mission Married Ladies' Sketch Party

Tram accident at Halifax, 1 July 1905

she took two backward paces, until at last she was brought to bay against the railings that front the school-house – and then she turned half-face to her tormentor, and sidled back along the railings, and pleaded shopping as an excuse for cutting short all further colloquy.

Then, had she no friends, this little old lady who detested men? To be sure she had – friends of the self-same fashion, who formed a Round Table of old maids, and who met constantly to discuss the weighty topics of the parish. Indeed, as we look back upon their tea-parties, and morning calls, and evening walks among their garden flowers, Bingley shows in a fresh guise altogether, as the Village of Old Maids. Where have they gone, these gentle maiden ladies, with their lavender, and mittens, and rustling gowns of silk? We meet none like them now – none with the same soft voices, the same well-bred avoidance of distasteful topics, the same quiet courage when courage is demanded. There is too little lavender grown nowadays in the world's gardens.

Halliwell Sutcliffe

'NO GOWK, BUT REAL SWADDLE'

Another interesting 'old habitant' is George Reynoldson, now in his 83rd year, who began work at the age of ten as a miner at 'T'owd Gang' mine, wherein he toiled for 63 years. George was summoned to London as a witness in regard to certain Shooting Rights – an action between the Lord of the Manor and the Broderick family, yeomen of Spring End and Summer Lodge. If we remember rightly, the trial ended in favour of the Lord of the Manor, although the Brad-rykes (Brodericks) lineage in the dale dated from, if not before, the Conquest. Another ancient witness was Jimmy Calvert, whose age was 90 years. To some question put by the judge to Reynoldson, anent shooting, he is said to have answered, 'Yer honour, it isn't shutting noo-a-days, its on'y modder (murder)! When ah wer a lad, gentlemen used to shut ower points (pointer-dogs) – that's wat a' call spoort. Noo-a-days, t' gents hire men to draave birds tit guns, which is nowt at all but modder.' George clearly proved a tough nut for the London barristers to crack – 'no gowk, but real Swaddle.' During his cross-examination he replied, hand to ear, 'A's varry deaf – ye mun speak up – ah ave already said all at ah noo t' t'other side, an' ye heeard it all, an' a've nowt else to tell ye.' To the writer's question, 'And what did you think of London?' he made answer, 'Ah reckon nowt at all aboot Lunnon – they're onny pupheeads there; it's a faane place eneaf, bud theer's sadly too mich sparkling abaat. Kristle Pallace is a faane place, an' might dea (do) well eneaf. There was lots a portraits of kings and queens' which seems to have pleased the old fellow mightily; but 'the finest place on earth' to George's thinking is Melbecks Moor and T'owd Gang Mines!

Edmund Bogg

The lighthouse at Withernsea

QUAKER HOSPITALITY

I was weather-bound one day in early summer at a town a little west of [Swaledale]. Late in the afternoon, tired of watching the heavy showers blow past the windows, I started on my way; but the walk was wet and cheerless, and I was not sorry when a cart stopped by my side and the driver offered me a lift. I looked at him. He had a face of exceptional kindness, such as invited instant confidence even from a surly dweller in great cities; and I got into the cart and sat beside the tall old farmer with a sudden feeling that something warm and friendly had risen up out of the cold rain and clinging mist which were beating once again across the road.

In his slow way the old man insinuated many questions as to my journeys, and finding out at last that I was expected nowhere, his face broadened into a large smile, and he said, 'Then tha'll come hoam wi' me' with such an obvious delight in having found an unexpected guest that I had no mind to make excuses; and we drove away off the main road which I had been following, as friendly a pair of comrades as any in the north country.

He was a Quaker, the old man told me, and he had much to say about the decadence of that once numerous body of simple, upright men among the dales. The ancient meeting-houses rarely, on any first day, held more than a handful of worshippers, though he remembers them crowded. Presently we passed the meeting-house of his own village, a grey old building on the hillside, bearing an early seventeenth-century date above its little porch, and looking down the long valley through which we had come something in the manner of a sentinel set to watch. Almost in the bottom of the valley lay the old man's farm; and as we uncurled ourselves, cold and rather stiff, from our seats in the market cart, the house door opened, letting out a glow of light and warmth from a ruddy kitchen fire; and in the doorway, backed up by the bright reflections from pots and pans which shone like mirrors, stood a little rosy-cheeked old woman, clad in the grey shawl and spotless cap which still, in solitary places, proclaim the Quaker. The aged collie, who had risen slowly with a toothless bark of welcome, sniffed suspiciously about my heels; but the old woman beamed, and when her husband brought me up, saying, 'This is a friend, and he's coom to stay t' neet wi' us,' she held out her hand and shook mine warmly, saying, 'Thou art very welcome, friend;' and so took me in, a stranger, out of the wet evening into the warmth and light of her cheerful home.

Dear, kindly people! I can still see the little parlour lighted up, the great chair in which the farmer always sat drawn over to the hearth, and another smaller one set close by the arm. There, after a few vain efforts to ensconce me in the seat of honour, the old man placed himself with the comfortable action of a man who, after hard toil, finds himself resting in a familiar spot; and by his elbow sat his old wife knitting. 'She

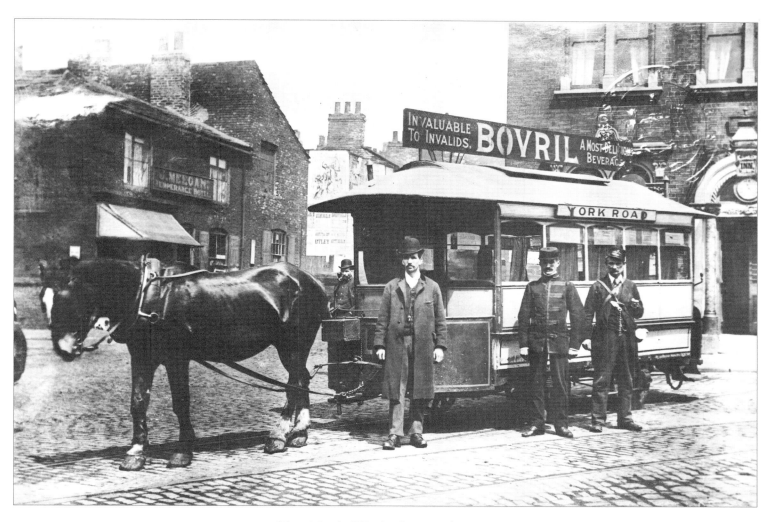

Tram No. 1, 'Woodpecker', Leeds, 1897

likes to sit there while I read,' he said, with a half suspicion that the propinquity might need some explanation to a stranger. As for the little Quakeress, she looked up and smiled without speaking, for it was not her habit to talk much.

So they sat all evening in the little dimly-lit room, while my host talked to me of the things which were next his heart. And so I see them still in my memory, sitting side by side in absolute content, a pair of happy, placid people, for whom life held no difficulties any more, and who had no wishes save to enjoy the evening of their days together. There were long tracts of silence, during which the old man lay back in his chair, and his wife looked up smiling as often as she caught my eye; and in the end a supper of milk and cheese was brought in, and I went to rest in a room where the old mahogany four-poster was polished like a mirror, where the sheets smelt of lavender, and a lilac bush beneath the lattice window filled the room with sweetness all the night.

Arthur H. Norway

A SHOCKING SLANDER ON YORKSHIREMEN

Long ago, in an old hotel in a midland county, where the landlord gratified a sporting taste by collecting any work of art which dealt with horses, or with pigs, for he combined both tastes, I saw a curious wooden panel, which the proud owner described to me as 'The Yorkshire Coat of Arms.' It was such a shocking slander that I hesitate to speak of it. Yet if people who are traduced do not hear what is said of them, how can they rebut the scandal? Shall I not therefore act the part of friendship, and repeat it?

This scurrilous old panel was shaped in the form of a shield, and as crest it bore a horse proper, the signification of which was that Yorkshire is the best county in which any man can buy a horse – which I make no doubt is perfectly true. But mark what followed – Ah! had the artist but only ended there. The shield was in four quarters, adorned respectively with a fly, a flea, a limpet and a piece of beef, and these enigmatical devices mine host explained gleefully as follows. 'A Yorkshireman,' quoth he, 'can drink like a fly, he can bite like a flea, he can stick fast like a limpet, and lastly, he is no good at all until he is hung.' There, – it was not I who said it! – is it not shameful and atrocious? Will not every Yorkshireman desire to find and burn this panel? It was in Warwickshire that I saw it. Let those who list take that cue, and search diligently till they find it.

Arthur H. Norway

Photographer Frank Meadow Sutcliffe's daughters, Kathy and Lulu, Whitby

Chapter 2

VOICES OF CHILDREN

'**M**y mother had been thrashing me. Made reckless by my fear of pain, I ran wildly round my bedroom, howling, trying to dodge the cane.' This is not the recollection of a child from some industrial slum in the West Riding: it comes from the novelist Storm Jameson's autobiography Journey from the North. Her family were impeccably middle class, living in a substantial house in the fashionable West Cliff district of Whitby.

Many other autobiographies of the time confirm that being beaten by one's parents was a daily possibility, often a probability, inflicting hurts that lasted a lifetime. Demonstrations of open affection, Christabel Burniston wrote, were 'rather like four-leaved clovers; more remarkable than the three-leaved variety because they were scarce'.

When one's schooling began, the physical assaults became if anything more frequent. In the classroom, the birch, the rod and the ruler were almost universally regarded as capital aids to the imparting of knowledge. Moreover, many teachers seemed to relish humiliating their charges, placing them in a corner wearing a dunce's hat or making them stand for an hour or more on a stool in front of the class as punishment for some minor peccadillo.

There were compensations of course. Children could be allowed to wander on their own through towns and countryside, or roll their hoops along main roads where a car was as rare a sight as an elephant or dancing bear. And despite the growing number of illegitimate births, most children enjoyed the security of two parents and a ramification of aunts, uncles, cousins and other sundry relatives.

The most telling difference in the childhood of one hundred years ago was the prevalence of death. Brothers and sisters routinely disappeared and their passing was often seen by parents as a relief. One writer, Maggie Joe Chapman, remembered her grandmother, a midwife, decrying a mother who had just given birth to a still-born baby. 'I nivver saw sike a set [such a fuss] as she's makkin' – Lord, it's a repairable loss!' That was what they thought of losing babies, 'a repairable loss'. And in Middlesbrough, Lady Bell records one mother, all of whose children had died, saying 'It is better they died, for I had them all insured'.

By contrast, it is a pleasure to read Christabel Burniston's account of her childhood in a suffragette family in Leeds and of her open-eyed delight in a visit to Messrs Marks & Spencer's dazzling Penny Bazaar with all of sixpence to spend as she chose.

Gillamoor Wesleyan Sunday School outing, 3 July 1913

In Boston Park, Rotherham

A MATCH, TO LIGHT IT THROUGH THE WORLD

Should the child be born with a caul, so much the better. It is a most lucky sign, though indicating the infant will become a wanderer. The caul should be dried and kept, as it will ensure its owner against death by drowning. Until after she has been churched, no newly made mother should enter a neighbour's house. If she be guilty of such injudiciousness, a baby will be born in the said house before a year passes. This will come true, even if the circumstances be most unlikely. An infant should 'be taken up before it is taken down.' If born in a top room, so as to make it impossible to carry it higher, then it must be held overhead by some one who is standing on a chair or table. A child born with teeth will die before it is a year old, so likewise will one who cuts the lower incisors first:–

> Quickly toothed, then quickly go,
> Quickly will your mother have moo.

If it lives – which is most unlikely – it will be different from other children. At the first house into which a baby is taken, the mistress must give it its blessing. The blessing is as follows:–

1. An egg, that it may never want meat.
2. Salt, (*a*) to savour that meat; (*b*) that it may never need friends.
3. Bread, that it may never want food.
4. A match, to light it through the world.
5. A coin, that it may never want money.

Infants should cry during the baptismal service, some people deliberately making them do so, in order that they 'may scream the devil out.' After the ceremony, the nurse must be supplied with 'a drop o' summat' with which to drink its health. This custom is called 'washing the baby's head.' The real washing of that part of its small person should not be attempted before the child is a year old, and then with whisky and water for the first time. Its nails should never be cut, but be bitten short instead. Should a child say 'mamma' first, there will soon be another; if 'dada,' there will be no other, or, at any rate, none before a long interval.

Miss M.W.E. Fowler

'A DIMPLE ON THE CHIN BRINGS A FORTUNE IN'

In the dales of Cleveland and Wensleydale, to guard her babe from the influence of evil spirits and bad wishes, the mother used to place a Bible under the pillow of the sleeping child, until such time as the infant had been christened, that being considered sufficient protection against all evil spirits. And in the days of witchcraft, in many houses where the first cradle would shortly be tenanted, it was most carefully kept wrong side up until the child was laid in it. This was done so that no other living thing in that house should sleep in it before the coming owner. Otherwise the cradle would be forestalled, and in after years the occupant might have reason to doubt the fidelity of his wife, or vice versa.

Unknown child photographed at Bradford

In such fear was this forestalling of the cradle held, that one was rarely purchased until absolutely needed. A cradle should always be paid for before it crosses the threshold. It is said that the child who sleeps in an unpaid-for cradle will end its days lacking the means to pay for its own coffin, or, as others put it, be too poor to pay for its lodgings on the earth or in it. Should the baby when grown older say 'Papa' before he or she utters 'Mamma,' then be assured the next little stranger will be a boy; however, should it say 'Mamma' first, then it will be a girl; and should it say 'Papa' and a girl is born, then be quite sure that it said 'Mamma' some little time before, when no one was near. This last bit is mine; I like to help even a superstition out of a difficulty.

If baby's first tooth appears in the upper jaw, it is not considered a good sign; there is a fear of the child dying in infancy. Sometimes they don't.

Should the baby be born with a mole on its chin, success is strongly foreshadowed; the same on the left thigh is considered quite the reverse. One on the right temple gives wealth and high position, and one placed at the outside corner of either eye denotes a sudden death. Whilst

A dimple on the chin brings a fortune in,
A dimple on the cheek leaves the fortune for to seek.

No woman ever dreamt of crossing any threshold but her own until after she had been churched, as in doing so she carried ill-luck into every house she entered.

Richard Blakeborough

'CUT 'EM O' FRIDAY, YA CUT 'EM FOOR SORROW'

The baby's nails must not be cut during infancy; should they grow inconveniently long, they may be bitten off by the mother, for if they were cut, the child would grow up light-fingered, i.e. a thief. When the child has celebrated its first birthday, they may be properly cut; but here again certain days must be avoided – Fridays and Sundays are considered to be very unlucky. It is a common saying –

Better t' baan 'ed ne'er been born,
'An cut its naals on a Sunday morn.

There is no virtue attached to the pieces of the nails when cut, but the first pieces bitten off should be carefully preserved, until there is a scrap from every nail on both hands; these must be wrapped together and buried under an ash-tree, and the child, if not freed from the diseases incident to the young, will only have them in a slight degree.

The old rhyme says–

Cut 'em o' Munday, cut 'em foor health;
Cut 'em o' Tuesday, cut 'em foor wealth;
Cut 'em o' Wednesday, cut 'em foor news;
Cut 'em o' Thorsday, ya cut foor new shoes;
Cut 'em o' Friday, ya cut 'em foor sorrow;
Cut 'em o' Seterday, t' bairn nivver need borrow;
Cut 'em o' Sunday, 't 'ed better be deead,
Foor ill-luck an' evil 'll lig on its heead.

Again:–

Sunday clipt, Sunday shorn,
Better t' bairn 'ed nivver been born.

Richard Blakeborough

CORRECT COLOURS FOR A SUFFRAGETTE BABY

I can see Nurse Malthouse now – although it can only be through photographs and her regular return visits – an imposing rigid figure wearing a long starched apron, stiff white cap clamped down to keep every hair out of sight, floor length navy and white-striped cotton dress, eight-inch-long stiffly starched white cuffs with gold cufflinks, and a huge wrist-watch completely encased in leather. It was a totally inappropriate garb for dealing with the sucking, spitting and exploding which punctuates a baby's life. The 'morning-daily' was faced not only with an extra baby's washing, including Turkish towelling nappies, but with Nurse Malthouse's daunting uniform.

Even though I was the fourth girl and money was short, my parents had not run out of names, and endowed me with the rather grand name of: Sarah Elizabeth Christabel Hyde, a splendid 4/4 rhythm which lent itself to doggerel verse and song.

The Dame School at Venom's Nick, Rosedale

On the beach at Bridlington

My mother was an ardent Suffragette, albeit a gentle one, who – I feel sure – in 1909 would rather have been carrying a banner than a baby. It was a critical year for the Suffragettes for, by this time, frustrated by the failure of persuasive protest to the Government, they mounted their military campaign. The eloquence of Mrs Emmeline Pankhurst and her daughter Christabel reached a peak. My mother sublimated her fervour, frustration and faith into christening her fourth daughter 'Christabel'.

My sisters told me that instead of the usual 'pink for a girl' I was decked out in the purple, white and green of the Suffragette movement, and that the white pillow of my pram was heavily appliquéd with purple clematis and green leaves. I still possess a piece of purple, white and green striped ribbon which, we were told, came direct from Christabel Pankhurst. Incongruously, my mother's dedication to the cause was interpreted in some rather twee feminine *objets d'art*: a large white satin tea cosy lavishly embroidered with purple irises and green leaves; white linen cone-shaped hair tidies with purple violets and green ribbons; needle-cases of white flannel with lavender covers and of course delicate white china cups with purple pansies, all presents, I should think, from some of the genteel passion-spent aunts.

Christabel Burniston

Artist's impression of Michael Marks' original stall in Leeds Market

AN OUTING TO MARKS & SPENCER'S PENNY BAZAAR

So the three of us set off for the tram. 'Please can we go on top?' I could see the sparks from the cable, look into people's bedrooms, hear the click and ring of the conductor's ticket machine on his belt. After three miles of clanging and riding there we were, straight opposite the glass arcade. And I could *read* it! 'Marks & Spencer's Penny Bazaar.' Gertie helped me on 'Admission' but we all chimed in on '*Free*'.

My hands were hot and sticky with clutching my sixpence in the pocket of my muff; the fear of losing it obsessed me.

When at last we went in, having savoured every possible thing outside, Ada said, 'What about changing your sixpence?' It sounded threatening to me. 'Ask the shop-lady if you can.' She didn't need asking: ''Ow'd you like it, luv?' she beamed. ''Ow many pennies? 'Ow many 'ay'pennies and 'ow many farthings?' I was considered bright for my age so I couldn't let Gertie and Ada down: 'Three pennies, four ha'pennies . . .' I hesitated, then I stumbled out: 'And the rest in farthings!'

Gertie and Ada beamed with pride and eleven bright gold new coins were in my hand. Too many to clutch. Far too many to spend! I pushed them into the red velvet poke in the lining of my fur muff. Gertie and Ada were just the right people for this store; the longer it took to spend sixpence the more their frugal minds were pleased.

Choosing was painfully exciting. The counters, tilted down from back to front, were packed – 'Don't ask the price – It's a penny!' There were cotton reels – enough colours for Joseph's coat – packets and books of needles from difficult-to-thread to crewel, pins on sheets, measuring tapes,

coathangers, hairpins, hair tidies. 'No need to make your choice yet' said Gertie, lifting me up to get a better view. On we went: combs, hair-brushes, sponge bags, shaving soap, shaving mugs . . . I chose a shaving stick in a wooden case which you could twist up and down. Gertie and Ada had to sniff their approval of the perfume. 'Lady-like' they agreed, which seemed odd for soap for my Daddy. It was wrapped up in brown paper, tied with string and handed over in exchange for my two ha'pennies. 'Ta, luv. Ta'Tah.'

On to the kitchen-ware: pots, pans, sieves, colanders, cups, jugs, teapots, slop basins . . . ; it was mind boggling. I daren't touch even though Ada held me up so that I could. Instead I just pointed to a little white jug with purple violets and green leaves. 'Your Mother will love those colours' they both said in chorus. They peered underneath. 'Real china too.'

Another penny bought an autograph album for Kathleen, with pages of pale blue, pink and green; a strap purse for Nancy with the other penny and a little black flat-iron for Betsy to iron her doll's clothes. And I still had four farthings in my pocket.

'Now my dear,' said Gertie, 'we think you should have the last penny to spend on yourself!' That crowned the day.

On to the counter of pencil boxes, pens, crayons, tubes of paint, rulers, waste paper baskets . . . I chose – and kept it for years – a shiny black hardbacked notebook with a metal pencil that fitted into a little groove with a *hundred* sheets for, it said on the outside, *Memorandum*.

A tall man came up to us in his black tail coat, grey-striped trousers, oiled hair and Kitchener moustache and addressed Gertie: 'Can I help you Madame?' 'No thank you,' said Gertie, 'we're just showing the child round before her parents come to buy.' Ada rubbed her hands nervously. 'Quite all right, Madam.' He bowed and glided away towards a lady in a velvet hat and fur coat . . .

Gertie and Ada had been whispering away above my head, but I did catch the last words: 'Let's take her; it's only threepence,' and I was whirled along into a cavern of snow-blue-white where the one and only Santa Claus beamed in the circle of white fur round his head. I was too excited and nervous to answer his questions but I came away with a parcel wrapped in red crinkly paper all tied up with silver ribbon. It was *mine*. This was not going in Ada's basket but into my muff. It was cold and blackly damp out in Boar Lane and the Town Hall clock boomed four times. The tram, trucks, carts and horses were deafening and I missed all of Gertie's and Ada's talk except: 'Annie did say we could . . . ' People seemed taller, heavier, darker, noisier . . . as we pushed our way through to what I now know was Bond Street and into Fuller's Café.

The sheer bliss of that pale blue, pale pink, pale grey room, warm with tea and toast, remains haloed in my memory. Veils were lifted, gloves removed, and the neatest of little waitresses in a frilled white cap and bibbed apron wrote our order down: 'Tea for two and an extra cup for the girl; two slices of coffee and walnut cake for my sister and I.' (Gertie thought 'I' was more refined than 'me'.) 'A doughnut for the child; she doesn't like nuts.' As we weren't allowed to *dis*like anything, I couldn't understand Gertie's mistake. Had it something to do, I thought years later, with the simple fact that doughnuts were a penny and the Fuller's famous walnut cake was tuppence a slice?

Gertie – for she was the natural tea-pourer – half filled my cup with milk and then added hot water. Gertie and Ada manipulated minute pieces of their cake on to minute forks – an operation new to me – after making sure that my doughnut was cut into inch-sized pieces. They dallied luxuriously, making a little go a long way. They sipped their tea with their little fingers poised in air so that the flowers and the gold rims of the teacups were not hidden.

'Another jug of milk, please, waitress, and a jug of hot water if you please.' The Town Hall clock struck five. 'It's very homey, isn't it, Ada?' I didn't quite understand. It didn't seem a bit like their home as I remembered it nor even mine. There was a whispering between Gertie and Ada as they worked out whether they should give the waitress one penny or two. 'She's been very obliging with the milk and the hot water and so nice to the child.' It was an intense moment. 'Let's make it tuppence. I'm sure Annie wouldn't mind.'

Out in the dark damp cold, the newspaper men were bawling out: 'Late Night Final, Late Night Final . . . ' and words I could not catch. 'Germans' . . . was the only word.

But whatever Gertie and Ada heard it quickened their steps: 'No, we're not wasting a ha'penny on an Evening Post. We don't want any bad news today – not fair to the child.'

(The 'child' only realised years later that what the men were shouting out on that magical day in December 1914 – such a lavish and loving day – was 'Scarborough shelled . . . one hundred dead, two hundred wounded'.)

Christabel Burniston

Scarborough after the bombardment of 16 December 1914

A 'WICKED' ESCAPE FROM DROWNING

The Esk was in spring flood, with a strong, fast current, and we amused ourselves on its bank until my sister lost her footing on a loose stone, and sank. I snatched at her desperately from the same jutting stone and dragged her out, drenched and shivering. We ran to a cottage, where a woman stripped her and dried her clothes.

For a week after this, to bring home to her the depth of her wickedness in coming within a hair's breadth of drowning, she was made to stand on a stool before the roomful of grinning children, every morning for an hour. She was five, a little less.

Storm Jameson

MARIANA AT THE GRANGE

One day my Father brought a delightful toy back from Northallerton: it was a small musical box which played 'For there's nae luck about the house'. But my Mother, perhaps then, or perhaps shortly afterwards, when there was sufficient cause, thought the tune was ominous. My only sister was a baby then, between two and three years old. Our Farm was called the Grange, and though it had no moat, this daughter was christened Mariana. Perhaps that too was ominous, for a sad song goes by her name. Mariana was fair as sunlight, and smiled to the tinkle of the musical box. And that is all I remember of her, for that Spring I was suddenly sent away. A few days later my Aunt told me that Mariana had become an angel, and the next time we went to Kirkdale I was taken to see the unmeaning mound that covered her body.

Herbert Read

A MOTHER 'OUT OF ALL PATIENCE'

In the spring of 1903 we were living in a newly-built house on the West cliff [Whitby], at that time two miles of fine turf, naked to the North Sea wind. The move brought us within hearing of the sea, close to the cliff-top and the zig-zag path leading to the sands. Not that we used it, preferring to climb down and up two hundred feet of slippery red clay and rocks. There was a very large yard at the back of the house, and my mother let me keep a young white rabbit a friend of hers offered me. She detested animals; when, in a week or two, I grew bored with looking after it she was thankful to give it away. No sooner had it gone than I was filled with remorse, imagining its grief at being unwanted, and weeping bitter tears which started again each time I recalled its trick of springing from the ground upright, like a dancer.

'You should have cared when you had it,' my mother said, with dry justice.

This house was two miles from our new school; we did the walk four times a day, always late and always running. We became known for the habit. We ran to dancing-class, to the

Mrs Annie Lyon, East Ayton

Spa fireworks and concerts, even, when we were alone, to church. No one was surprised to see us racing through the streets to my eldest aunt's funeral. She and my aunt Jane, eldest and youngest of the Gallilees, were the only ones not married, still living in the same house. My mother had gone early, leaving us to dress and follow. In the end we had to run like hares.

As it turned out, we need not have run. The funeral had been held up by the refusal of the undertaker's men to nail the coffin. Dr Mitchell had to be called to assure them that the old lady was dead: her gleaming white hair, rosy cheeks and wide-open blue eyes frightened them. Pray God she really was dead.

My mother this summer was out of all patience with her life, herself, us. She was going to have a child in November; she had not wanted another child, eight years after her son's birth, and her exasperation and weariness drove her to violent rages, which were really fits of despair.

During these weeks I went through a crisis of anxiety about her. Farther back than I can remember, this irrational anxiety had been growing in me: it now reached a desperate climax. It woke me at night and sent me creeping downstairs from my room on the top floor to crouch outside the door of her bedroom: I sat there for two, three, four hours, until I was chilled to the bone, then went back

Summer holiday at Bridlington

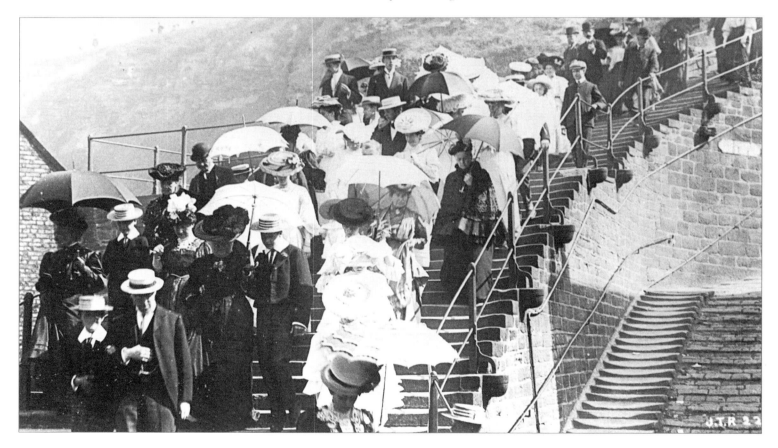

The 101 steps at Whitby after Sunday morning service

to bed and fell asleep. During the days, too, when she locked herself in her room, to endure, out of our sight, the unhappiness we did not – how could we? – understand, I couldn't bring myself to carry away the tray of food she refused, but waited outside with it uselessly for an hour before giving up.

One evening when my mother was leaving the house in anger after a quarrel, I asked her when she would be back.

'Never!' she said drily.

I was much too young to reflect that one does not leave home for ever on foot, without so much as a dressing-case. In despair, I followed her. She took a road that after four miles or so would bring her to Aislaby moor, and we walked for an hour or longer, I keeping myself, as I imagined, out of sight. At last she turned round, took my hand, and we went back together, in the gathering darkness, in silence.

I shudder now when I think what unhappiness that silence of hers hid.

Storm Jameson

TOP OF FATHER'S EGG FOR A TREAT

It was at Thackley that we became conscious that we were poor. Five growing children must have taken some feeding in any case. Scrag end of mutton and dumplings for dinner, fried bread and tea-gravy (made by pouring tea into the bacon dip in the frying pan) for breakfast with an occasional top of father's egg as a treat (which we had to take in turns), bread and margarine and treacle at tea-time, and at supper time a few grape-nuts in a saucer with a little drop of milk, or bread and dripping and a cup of cocoa – these were the meals I chiefly remember. Talking of milk, it didn't of course come in bottles, but the milkman used to call each morning with his large covered pail to which were hooked measures of various sizes. Mother, I remember, was often perturbed when in the cold weather the milkman would sometimes have a dewdrop on the end of his nose, and we would watch fascinated to see if it would drip into the milk!

When we children said we were hungry mother would fetch the Zweilback, which was made from any left over bits of bread and crusts baked in a tin that lived permanently on the bottom shelf of the oven until they were brown and brickhard. I never liked the stuff but it was something to chew.

Daisy Burton

POSITIVE BENEFITS FROM A CHILD'S DEATH

One's first impression is that when the question is asked of the mother in one of these cottages, 'How many children have you?' the answer one fears always comes, 'I have had' so many; 'I have buried' so many.

We must remember also that the number of children who die is – in some cases, at any rate, not to say in many –

Milk delivery boy, Whitby

due to the fact that the child's life has been insured; for many a time the parent is acutely conscious that it lessens the burden of life on the whole that instead of there being another child to look after, its place should be empty and some additional funds come in to compensate for its loss. One woman whose child had just died said in reply to condolence that 'it would not have mattered so much in another week, as by then the insurance would have come in.' Another spoke almost flippantly about all her children dying, and said, 'It is better they died, for I had them all insured.' This, perhaps, can hardly be wondered at, when one considers what the constant physical strain must be, in the case of a large family, merely to keep the children alive. To the weak and ailing mother the child is looked upon often as more of a trouble than a joy, and if insured its death is a positive benefit instead of a misfortune. It is allowed to die, therefore, without making much effort to keep it.

Lady Bell

Miss Mackenzie's cookery class, Kirkham Lane School, Pickering

SAD AFFAIR AT THE MIDDLESBROUGH WORKHOUSE

A Girl Drowned in the Bath

On Friday night a deep gloom was cast over the workhouse at Linthorpe by a sad and painful occurrence; a young girl named Jane Wilson, aged eight years, being drowned in the large bath while a number of others were bathing, without the knowledge of anyone at the time. Perhaps the most painful part of the unfortunate affair was the discovery of the body at the bottom by another bather. It appears that between seven and eight o'clock on Friday night the deceased was bathing in the large bath at the workhouse with a number of other girls, one of whom named Geddes placed her on the steps at the shallow end of the bath, and, telling her to remain there, went away. Shortly afterwards another girl named Rowe kicked against something at the deep end of the bath, and on looking found it was the deceased, who, when taken out, was dead.

Middlesbrough Daily Exchange, *3 March 1887*

Idle youths at Toll Gravel, Beverley

The Gardens, Ilkley

In Dentdale

Chapter 3

STRANGE CUSTOMS AND RARE BELIEFS

'*T*he social life of rural England is still largely governed by the moon' noted J. Fairfax-Blakeborough, a prolific chronicler of the folklore and customs of late nineteenth-century Yorkshire. 'Dances, parties, concerts and meetings are fixed for a night on which "there is a moon" to light home those who have to travel along dark lanes and moorland roads.' Farmers would only sow corn when the moon was waxing and 'we never have our pigs killed unless the moon is filling'.

In the remote communities of the Dales and the scattered villages of the East Riding, the existence of witches and their ability to turn themselves into hares was regarded as a matter of fact. Anyone believed to have the Evil Eye led a miserable existence, their fellow-villagers avoiding eye-contact and crossing the street lest a stray, baleful glance should blight their lives. At Staithes, the Revd A.N. Cooper was horrified by the fishermen's superstition that it was unlucky to save a drowning man. 'The old people could tell tales of men nearly dragged ashore, and then, by the advice of their elders, abandoned to their fate lest ill-fortune should result from saving them.'

More innocuous beliefs were listed by the hundred: 'Should a hairy worm cross your path, pick it up, throw it over your shoulder and wish', 'Wet your finger and cross your left shoe and wish every time you see a piebald horse'. It was not just the uneducated who subscribed to such 'rare beliefs'. The Revd J.C. Atkinson, Rector of Danby in the North York Moors, had met 'any number of cultured people who devoutly believe that suffering the sun to shine freely upon a fire in the ordinary grate puts it out; that setting a poker vertically up against the fire grate in front of it, causes the smouldering, nearly extinct fire to burn brightly up'.

The late nineteenth century saw a revival of interest in old customs. Some had never lapsed: the tolling of the curfew bell at Richmond, and the Town Watchman in Ripon Market Place winding four blasts on his horn each evening dated back to medieval times. Others, like Morris dancing and May Day festivities were somewhat artificially resuscitated. According to Thomas Hardy, you could tell which were the genuine survivals because everyone taking part in those had an expression of performing a rather wearisome duty. And one custom whose passing few regretted was 'Riding the Stang', an act of vigilante thuggery described in this chapter by J. Fairfax-Blakeborough.

Cyclists' fancy dress competition, Ripon, c. 1899

'Chapping a frontiersman', Scarborough

HOW TO FRUSTRATE A WITCH

Witch Wood

This has ranked amongst the most important factors used in trying to frustrate the plottings of the witch.

Collecting their stocks of witch wood was an undertaking not to be lightly entered into. Several observances had to be carried into effect. For instance, the branches of the rowan tree must be cut off by no other means than a household knife and from a tree that was entirely unknown, even if they had to go a long distance to find such a one, as all rowan trees growing on their own farms would be familiar to them, and that would not do. After finding a tree answering all these requirements, and securing a sufficient stock of it to meet all necessities, they must by no means return home with it by the same way in which they went. Last, but not least of the precautions taken in order that it might have the full prophylactic efficacy desired, the wood must on no account be cut and gathered on any other day than St Helen's Day. As already stated, many and varied were the offices the witch wood was called upon to fulfil. One piece was to be placed at the head of the beds, others to be carried in the trousers pockets, pieces for the dairy, and like uses. No man would think of taking horses and wagons on the roads without taking along also the rowan-tree gad, a long straight sapling grown from the roots of the rowan tree, in place of a whip. These were all preliminary measures taken with a view of protecting themselves from the spells of the witch, but, in spite of all, cattle would die and all sorts of untoward happenings would occur.

Joseph Ford

A CHARM AGAINST THE AGWORM

The writer has in his possession a small piece of hazel wood, about six inches in length and much the same as a stick of lead pencil in diameter. This insignificant twig or piece of wood has been part of a small branch, as is shown by the fact of its still retaining the bark.

It was believed by the people of our Danby Parish that the wood possessed some mysterious charm in healing or curing the stings or bite of the Agworm (Adder), which eighty or ninety years ago were very numerous on the moors and in the fields adjoining. Adders are by no means extinct yet, for

Empire Day, Sheffield, 1906

we hear of farmers killing odd ones almost every year, especially when we get spells of hot weather, but they are seldom seen in the lower parts of the valley. Their native place seems to be the moors, or the fields adjoining the moors.

This small piece of wood, which came into my possession about fifteen years ago, was known throughout our parish and the dales around as Sowley's Irish Stick, as it was owned by the Sowley family for some generations, when it became widely known. When Agworms (the local name for Adders) were more numerous than they are now it frequently happened that cows or other livestock got stung with them. Shepherds often found their sheepdogs stung or bitten by adders, and in many ways the need arose for a charm. People came from far and near to borrow Sowley's Irish Stick, which the family were always pleased to lend, on the understanding that it was to be returned without delay after it had done its miraculous healing, because on the morrow they might want it themselves – they could never be sure.

Joseph Ford

HOW TO GET RID OF A SWALLOWED NEWT

Internal pains are frequently said to be caused by some animal which 'hez gotten hinside of a man.' In many cases it is known how this unfortunate state of things came about, and the unwelcome presence can be readily accounted for by the patient and his friends. A lad, when drinking from a pond, swallowed an 'askard' (newt). The boy saw 'its great eyes' just as it went in at his mouth, but before he could raise his head, the newt had slipped down his throat. For years afterwards he was troubled with symptoms resembling those of acute dyspepsia, till at last an old woman told him of a cure. He was to sit with his mouth wide open in front of a basin of hot bread and milk, the smell of which would tempt the askard out of his 'in'ards.' The cure was tried, and proved most successful. The askard simply rushed up his throat into the basin, after which the youth ceased to be troubled and lost all his former pains and discomfort. Another man had 'an askard or summat arkard' inside him, which was tempted out by hot beefsteak. At once it began to run round the table. Unfortunately the many onlookers tried to catch it, whereupon it jumped down the man's throat again. A woman gave the following story to account for her attacks of spasms: 'It be a fummard (weasel) as troubles me. It got into me when I were a gal, and t'way it gnaws at me hinside is hawful. There be nowt as 'ill kill it, an' its growed so sin' it went darn 'at no amount o' nothink can bring it up now!' She also believed her father's deafness was caused by an animal in his head, and used to tell of how, 'one fall,' he was lying asleep by the pond, during which time an askard must have crept in at his ear. 'E's been deaf ivver sin', and will be till e' can get shut on it.'

Miss M.W.E. Fowler

TELLING THE BEES

Around the district also linger many old-world legends and superstitious customs, such as putting the bees into mourning. On the death of a member of the household, the event is announced to the hive, which is draped with crape, and the bees served with biscuits soaked in wine; the ritual is known as 'telling the bees,' and should the practice be neglected, it is firmly believed the bees will die. Striking the door key on the fire shovel is a sure expedient to bring back to the hive a swarm of bees. Death warnings, mysterious signs and omens, etc: – a swarm of bees alighting on a dead branch is an unlucky omen, and sure sign of death in the family; children born at midnight are supposed to see 'doubly,' that is, have vision in darkness as well as in light, and are known as double or second sighted.

Edmund Bogg

LORE OF THE WART-CHARMERS

Wart-charmers are not defunct yet. I know several who, after pronouncing an inaudible incantation, rub the wart with a special stone, and then you are assured the wart or warts will die. Frog spit rubbed on a wart is said to be a certain cure. If you rub your wart with a black snail, sticking the snail on a thorn where you will never see it again, the wart, as the snail dies, will disappear. If you yearn to afflict any one with warts, let them wash in water in which eggs have been boiled. This belief is quite common to-day. A plate of salt, upon which a dead man's hand has rested overnight, used to be considered good for chilblains.

Richard Blakeborough

SOVEREIGN REMEDIES FOR A COUGH

Speaking of whooping cough, I remember a lady at Guisborough, only a few years ago, taking both her boys to the gasworks for them to inhale the fumes from the gas-tank. It nearly poisoned the whole three, but the cough survived it nicely. However, that and the field-mouse were infinitely preferable to the recipe I had from an old dame, who assured me 'no cough o' no kind whatsoever could stan' agaan it.' It was this: equal quantities of hare's dung and owl's pellets – the latter are the disgorged remains of feathers, bones, &c., which the owl objects to digest. Well, having carefully mixed

Market Square, Guisborough, c. 1895

these two ingredients with dill-water, clay, and the blood of a white duck, the resulting filth had to be made into pills the size of a nut, three of which had to be taken fasting on going to bed. This was to be continued until the cough was cured or the patient buried. A much simpler method is to catch a frog, open its mouth and cough into it three times, throw the poor brute over your left shoulder, and the patient will be cured at once. If not, depend upon it there is some very good reason why the charm has failed. One woman I knew, used to take her little girl and hold her over an old well when a bad fit of coughing seized the child. She declared, if at the time either a frog or a toad happened to be at the bottom of the well with its mouth open, the child would be cured instantly. I offered to catch her a frog and open its mouth for the child to cough into; this she objected to, because, as she said, the frog might spit at it and injure it for life. This belief in the poisonous and spitting power of frogs is still retained by the good people of Great Ayton, and also of many other places. I remember an old angler once saying to me, 'Ya see, the Lord gav' t' fishes understan'ing; tha knaw 'at frogs is venomous, an' tha're a gran' bait foor pike, bud neea pike'll tak ho'd if ya deean't run t' heuk thruff baith ther lips, seea ez tha can't spit at 'em.' 'But,' said I, 'how do the pike catch them when they are swimming in a natural state?' 'Easy eneeaf,' answered he: 'tha tak hodden 'em fra behint, an' tha can't spit backkards waay ower ther heeads, ya knaw.'

Still another plan may be tried to ease the little sufferers. If they be passed nine times under the belly and over the back of either a piebald pony or an ass (the latter preferred), the cough will be immediately charmed away, whilst a touch on the larynx from the hand of a seventh son of a seventh son is held to be a certain cure. And a hairy caterpillar or small wood-lizard tied round the child's neck, having been stitched in a small bag, was, and I believe is yet, looked upon as a sovereign remedy.

Richard Blakeborough

The maypole at Barwick-in-Elmet

the process (needing quite two hundred willing arms) is worse than lamed for life. As a Keswick rustic phrased it, to a friend of the writer, explanatory of an imbecile son, and gravely as of an indisputable truth, 'He got knocked at Barwick' (*i.e.*, with the Maypole) 'and was silly ever after.' 'Knocked at Barwick' is a saying for miles around when speaking of a person with weak intellect.

Edmund Bogg

'KNOCKED AT BARWICK'

Barwick still retains its Maypole and customs associated therewith; it is renewed every third year. The rearing of the pole is made the scene of great rejoicing and festivity; from city, town, and village, crowds of people pour in and help to swell the tumult and babel. The echoes of the past are reawakened, and Barwick, as of old, is, on these occasions, truly the capital of Elmet. Midway between the high mound and the stately church, the Maypole is upreared; in close proximity stands the base and portion of shaft of the market cross.

A very suggestive superstition clings to this Maypole, though, perhaps, to those in other places as well; this is, during the uprearing, the timber mast (spirally striped in colours symbolic of red blood and white may – the renewal of life) has a baleful quality about it, as it were, the personified evil of a Pagan idol; and whoever is struck by it in

INFLUENCE OF THE MOON

Those of us who live amongst the hills and moors (in semi-civilisation, in the opinion of townsfolk), know how great and potent a part the moon plays in influencing many of our operations. From the earliest appearance of each new moon it is invested with power for good or evil, over our lives. If we first see it through glass, ill-luck will be ours. We must first salute it out of doors, and with due respect. Males raise their hats and females curtsey their homage.

There are many farmers who to this day will not sow corn when the moon is waning, and we never have our pigs killed unless the moon is filling, in view of the common belief that bacon put down in salt when the moon is waning will not cure satisfactorily.

J. Fairfax-Blakeborough

Vicar Lane slaughterhouse, Leeds

BURYING THE ABORTIVE CALF

It is not unusual on a farm for one of the cows to give birth to a calf prematurely, in which case it often happens that the others in the cow byre follow suit, causing great loss to the farmer. In order to prevent the further dread loss, the abortive calf became at once the cause for putting into practice the old prophylactic or preventative in such a contingency.

First the doorstep of the cow byre in which the calamity had occurred had to be removed, and a very deep hole dug. Into this hole the abortive calf was laid on its back, the legs straight upright in the rigidity of death, then the earth was filled in and the stone step replaced in its former position. The main object of this story relating to the burying of the abortive calf is to draw attention to the fact that it was carried out on one particular farm in our Parish about the year 1918. There is evidence of its being resorted to at an even later date at a place not far removed from our parish, while yet another man who is still living can testify to taking part in this ancient practice.

Joseph Ford

A FAMOUS BOGLE

The subject of bogles is a tempting one, and I would fain linger on it in this region where they are so numerous. One famous member of the clan dwells at Runswick, whither I am going as fast as the hilly road permits, or rather he did dwell there until men quarrying for jet tore down the cliffs and destroyed the hole in which he used to lurk, reviled because he was fond of drowning people, yet loved because he cured them of the whooping-cough. Runswick is still what it always has been, a mere fishing village.

> 'Souther, wind, souther,
> And blow father home to mother;'

so the children used to chant while dancing on the cliff-top; and though they have grown too wise to do it in these days of Board schools, that is not because their hearts are set less eagerly on the changes of the sea, or the prospects of the fishing grounds. The houses are dotted here and there on the

Dorothy Taylor baiting lines at Runswick Bay, c. 1880

high broken ground which sweeps down in fine undulations to the shore, where two or three small boats lie hauled up on the beach, and a few low shelves of blackened rock jut out into the receding water. Cloud and sunshine sweeping over red rock and grey sea, the heavy blows of a caulking hammer resounding from a hillock just above the beach, the cries of children playing near the water's edge – such are the memories which I retain of Runswick Bay, a pleasant solitary spot unto this hour, and one which somewhat stirs the imagination by the very aloofness from the outer world which distinguishes it yet.

Gordon Home

The staff of the Co-operative Wholesale Society, Wetherby

RIDING THE STANG

A very old custom, but which has now been pretty nigh stamped out by the county policeman, is that of 'Riding the Stang.' It is not dead yet, though; I witnessed the stang being ridden as recently as 1891 in Guisborough, and in many of the villages in Wensleydale it is to this day resorted to when considered needful.

The stang is held in wholesome dread by a certain class of evil-doers. Wife-beaters and immoral characters chiefly had and have the benefit of the stang. Whatever their discovered sin might be, was fully set forth in the stang doggerel. One or two points have to be, or at least are, most carefully observed: (1) The real name of the culprit must not be mentioned. (2) The stang must be ridden in three separate parishes each night; and in many places, to make the proceedings quite legal, it was considered a *sine qua non* that the stang-master must knock at the door of the man or woman they were holding up to ridicule, and ask for a pocket-piece, i.e. fourpence.

The whole proceeding was carried out as follows:– An effigy made of straw and old clothes, representing the culprit, was bound to a pole [cow-staff] and set in an upright position in the centre of either a handcart or a small pony cart, in which was seated the stang-master; and following behind were gathered all the ragamuffins of the village, armed with pan lids, tin cans, tin whistles, or anything which could be made to produce a discordant sound. Being ready, the cart was drawn in front of the culprit's house, and after a fearful hubbub, the stang-master cried out, in a sing-song voice, –

Ah tinkle, Ah tinkle, Ah tinkle tang,
It's nut foor your part ner mah part
'At Ah rahd the stang,
Bud foor yan Bill Switch whau his weyfe did bang,
Ah tinkle, Ah tinkle, Ah tinkle, tang.
He banged her, he banged her, he banged her indeed,
He banged her, he banged her, afoor sha steead need;
Upstairs aback o' t' bed
He sairly brayed her whahl sha bled,
Oot o' t' hoos on ti t' green,
Sikan a seet ez nivver war seen,

Ez neean c'u'd think, ez neean c'u'd dream.
Sae Ah gat ma a few cumarades
Ti traal ma aboot;
Sae it's hip hip hurrah, lads,
Set up a gert shoot,
An' blaw all yer whistles,
Screeam, rattle, an' bang
All 'at ivver ya've gitten,
Foor Ah ride the stang.

Then, for a few moments, there arose a tumult of sound, to which the wildest ravings of bedlam would seem insignificant.

This performance lasts three nights, and on the third the effigy is burnt in front of the culprit's house.

Richard Blakeborough

THE DECLINE OF ST VALENTINE'S DAY

Of St Valentine's Day we might truly write, 'Poor St Valentine! for with thee it is Ichabod.' No longer do we find shop windows filled with works of art, wrought in silver, lace, and gold; no longer within a coral bower, hung with icicles and rosebuds, is the maiden's hand clasped or waist encircled; no longer does a pathway of powdered fish-scales lead direct to the little church seen in the far distance, whilst the overfed cupid, who managed to sit on the edge of a very thin cloud, must have fall'en off and decamped with the couple of skewered hearts which were usually floating at their own sweet will 'mid heaven. Hearts are at a discount now. Fifty years ago, love-making was a very real and somewhat pedantic proceeding; in these days, when time is money, the whole thing has been curtailed. It is – cut the dialogue and come to the bank book.

Why, there was a time, and only a few years ago, when as many pounds were spent on these love tokens as pennies now.

Richard Blakeborough

Market Place, Richmond

THE CURFEW TOLLS AT RICHMOND

The square is almost empty. The few honest citizens who stand about in knots are, I presume, waiting only till the 'gathering bell' booms out from the tower to break off their gossip and go home to bed. Eight sounds from the steeple. At the fourth stroke a little old man comes scurrying round the corner and rushes into the belfry door. He has hardly whisked his body out of sight when the last stroke sounds, and on that instant the sonorous clanging of the curfew peals out over the old town, a little wild and unsteady at the first, as if the guiding intelligence that grasped the rope was a trifle out of breath, but settling down to a deep, solemn note, which resounds over the empty market-place, and strikes upon my ear with all the lost significance of past days. But the worthy citizens of Richmond heed it not one whit. Their talk, their very jests go on unbroken, without even a glance at the belfry. Not one evinces the least desire to go home to bed; and even a party of small children playing hopscotch treat the mediaeval admonition with true modern contempt.

Gordon Home

HOW LONG BEFORE I MARRY?

There is no difficulty in obtaining information touching the time you will be married. Simply let an anxious maiden take a looking-glass, and an apron which she has never worn or held between herself and the light, into the garden when the moon is at full; she must be careful not to look upon the queen of night until the rites are concluded. Keeping her back, then, to the moon, let her stand upon something she has never stood upon before – a newspaper, an old box, anything – and drawing the apron over the glass, hold it so that the moon shines upon it; let her now count the number of moons she sees reflected through the apron, and so many years will it be before the happy day arrives. I may mention, if such a one is in any violent hurry to get married, it is best to choose the apron of some light material, and to draw it tightly over the glass; careful attention to these small details has a marvellous tendency to lessen the number of moons.

Richard Blakeborough

ESSENTIAL RULES FOR A WEDDING

It is unlucky to marry and not change the surname, for 'To change the name and not the letter, is a change for worse and not for better.' When the wedding day comes, care must be taken that the bride does not see the bridegroom before she enters the church. Though not of necessity seen, still she must wear something blue, and must remember that green is a colour to avoid. It is always unlucky to turn back when leaving home, but never more so than on the wedding day. If a return is inevitable, the misfortune can be minimised by sitting down on the first seat seen. The men

Mr and Mrs Holmes after their wedding in Hull, with bridesmaid and pageboy, 1906

of the wedding party sometimes leave the church early, in order to reach the girl's home before her return. This is known as 'running for the bride-door,' and the man who reaches it the first must be presented with a flower from the bouquet, or some other thing which the bride has had with her during the service. In the rougher parts, there is a race among the men, it being understood that the winner may claim and himself remove the bride's garter for a prize. On her return from church she must hide her gloves, in order that, after her departure, the bridesmaids may hunt for them, she who finds them being looked upon as the next to marry. The cake should be cut over the bride's head, 'for luck,' after which she must give her special friends crumbs 'to dream on.' These morsels are first passed through her wedding ring, care being taken that the ring does not come off during the process. It is admissible to drop it to the tip of the finger, holding it there with the thumb while manipulating the cake with the other hand. Each receiver makes her portion into a small parcel and hides it away till night. She must walk upstairs backwards to bed, place the cake under her pillow, tie her garters round the left bedpost, and get into bed backwards. All this without speaking. Whoever is dreamt of will be the future husband. On waking (if it be after midnight), she must sit up and eat the cake, at the same time wishing three wishes, which, if kept secret, will come true during the year.

Miss M.W.E. Fowler

A GOLDEN WEDDING SPEECH

Here is a golden wedding story. It was the village blacksmith's. He and his wife, after fifty years' married life had gathered all their children and grandchildren in the big kitchen. After a hearty meal and lots of reminiscences of old times, the good old blacksmith had to make a speech. This is what he said, 'Well, friends, we're right glad to see you. I've never made a speech in my life, but they tell me I've got to make one now. All I can say is that mother and me have lived together now for fifty years, and I can tell you this – if I'd all t' basketful to choose from again I should just pick t' same potato. I hope you'll all enjoy yourselves, and now I'll sit me down.'

C.J.F. Atkinson

A WORKING-CLASS WEDDING DAY

The young man of the iron-working class usually has no misgivings about embarking upon matrimony early and without a sufficient income. He marries very young, often because he wants a home of his own. Either he is in his parents' home, where he is of course not the principal person to be considered, and is set on one side perhaps and has to undergo the discomfort and crowding entailed by being one of a family living in a small cottage; or he is a lodger, under

Robert Collyer's smithy in Ilkley, 1868

much the same conditions. He marries a girl as young as himself, without in most cases either of them having any preconceived idea of what their life is going to be like, the responsibilities it will entail, or how to meet them. During their courtship they go about together in the streets, for the conditions are usually not favourable or agreeable within doors. I knew one mother whose supervision of her daughter took the strange form of saying she would not have the young man in the house, because, she said, she 'did not like such carryings on,' and she therefore let the girl walk about the streets with him often until midnight. It is not a state of things which is conducive to morality. They 'walk out' together, they fall in love, they have their brief romance. Then these two young people, with the equipment, or rather want of it, for the fight of life that I have described, embark on matrimony, and go into housekeeping on perhaps 23*s* or 24*s* a week, or even less. On the wedding-day the parents of the bride do not generally go to the church: sometimes the mother remains at home to superintend the cooking of the wedding feast; sometimes she is simply too busy to go out, and the wedding is merely an incident in the daily work. The young man and the young woman go off together to church with another man and girl, who fulfil the functions of groomsman and bridesmaid respectively. They either go on foot, or, if they can afford it, in a four-wheeled cab; and after the wedding is over they go back to their own house, and either have a day off and enjoy themselves, or else the man goes straight back to his work and the wife to her new home.

Lady Bell

SOME MEMORABLE FUNERALS

Funerals used to be great institutions in the dales. As many of the mourners had long journeys, it was a reasonable custom to provide them with a hearty meal at the house. Then these gatherings gave an opportunity of meeting the decreasing number of other old friends and relatives, to exchange news of one another and their families.

Though the dalesmen have deep feelings, they rarely show them, indeed they take a pride in concealing them – sometimes too much so. A friend of mine, when attending the funeral of a much respected farmer, spoke to the eldest son, expressing his sympathy, and said how much his father was thought of, and how he would be missed. The son, not from want of feeling, but just from want of power to express it, merely said, 'Ay, it's a bit orkard, isn't it?'

Another man returning from the burial of a friend said, 'It has been a good funeral, I bought four cows as we were walking to t' cemetery and back.'

At the funeral of a young farmer, I spoke to his brother, as we walked to the church, and expressed some sympathy and concern for the widow. The brother replied, 'Well, she's a very nice young woman, and I should think she'll soon get a second husband – let's hope so.'

Many years ago I heard this matter-of-fact outlook expressed in another way. One of the old-fashioned little Friendly Societies had got into financial difficulties, and the president consulted me. I advised that they should amalgamate with some larger society, and so make their sick benefits and funeral benefits, etc., safer. They were too small

Whit Monday festival at Sheffield

to create a sufficient reserve. I mentioned the name of one large and solvent organisation. He replied, 'Oh, I think nowt o' them! They only pay for burying one wife. Now our Lodge will let me bury as many wives as I can wed.' Further argument was useless. Soon afterwards the Society had to be wound up.

Once, whilst waiting in a barber's shop – that unofficial news-office of every country town – I was surprised by the appearance of two well known loungers who were, for them, exceptionally well dressed. The barber stayed his razor, looked them up and down, then said, 'Nay, ye've gotten 'em all on this time. What hev yer been doing?'

'We've been burying a chap ower at Yeadon.'

'Oh! Who've yer been burying?'

'Nay, lad, I've clean forgotten his reight name, but, by Gow, we hev' had some ale an' some eytin'. We hev' an' all.'

C.J.F. Atkinson

'GIT ON WI' THI DEEING'

A burly John Bull-like farmer lay a-dying. One of his visitors, a neighbouring farmer, said, before leaving the bedside, on one occasion very near the end:

'Noo, John, you must try and hang on a bit longer. You know it's a longish step to the churchyard, you'll be a bonny weight, and likely I'll be yan of your bearers, so hang on a bit longer. I can see you've lost a bit of flesh, but there's nowt like being bedfast for takkin' flesh off; now hang on a while longer.'

An old farmer on the moorlands, who was 'at the far end' was, as used to be the general custom with those *in extremis*, brought downstairs to die. There was a current idea that lying on feathers (particularly pigeon feathers) made it difficult for the soul to leave the body, and protracted the agony of death. So the old man was laid on 'the squab' (settle) in the kitchen, in which were assembled a number of relatives who had been summoned.

The old woman of the house was discussing the division of the furniture, and there was disagreement as to who should have the grandfather clock and a silver tea-caddy. The argument was interrupted by the dying man, who ventured to express his wishes regarding the disposal of the clock and caddy. However, his wife turned round and said:

'Thoo git on wi' thi deeing! We'll do t' talking and arranging things!'

J. Fairfax-Blakeborough

A COFFIN BORNE BY CHILDREN

. . . the coffin is never borne on the shoulders of the bearers, as is most customary elsewhere. So far as it is 'carried by hand' at all – which, from the distance of the church from all the constituents of the population, is very

Master S. Bullock, photographed at Harrogate, 4 June 1893

little, usually only from a few yards outside the churchyard-gate to the trestles set to support it in the western part of the nave of the church – it is carried by the aid of towels knotted together and passed under the coffin, the ends on either side being held by the bearers, six in number (or three pairs). And as regards the bearers, the usage was so consistent and so steadfast that there would be no impropriety in speaking of it as 'the rule.' Thus a single woman was borne by six single young women, a single young man by six of his compeers, a married woman by married women, and so on all through. Nay, it is no unusual sight even yet to see the child carried by six children, varying according to the sex of the dead child. In the case of the young unmarried woman, moreover, some peculiarities of costume were always to be observed about the bearers. Their dress was not all unrelieved black. White sashes or scarfs were customarily worn, and white gloves always. Much of this remains still, but the observance in such matters is hardly so religious as it used to be.

Canon J.C. Atkinson

The Floral Pavilion, Prince's Parade, Bridlington

Sheep washing at Fylingdales

Chapter 4

COUNTRY LIFE

'From the beams hung the bacon and the hams which the dalesman regards as the best decoration for any room.' Harry J. Scott's memories of a Yorkshire farmhouse at the turn of the century reinforce the nostalgic images of the idyllic, innocent way of life shown in the photographs throughout this book.

Most Yorkshire villages then had a smaller population than in 1800. The vast migration of labour to the manufacturing centres meant that, by 1900, less than 30 per cent of the population was living in the countryside. The North Riding, England's fourth largest county, had a population of fewer than half a million – and 20 per cent of them were crowded into the county's only industrial centre, Middlesbrough. The remaining 400,000 were scattered thinly across an area that stretched from what was then called the German Sea to within a few miles of Morecambe Bay.

In these vast open spaces, Dr R.W.S. Bishop noted that 'there is so much elbow-room for everybody that individual eccentricities are accentuated and the edges of character become sharp and rugged'. And because the communities were so small, 'Everybody knows everything about everybody and seeks to know more'.

Strait-laced Victorian morals became strangely distorted here. A village schoolmistress who had become pregnant by 'a heartless scoundrel' was dismissed 'for the good of the children', but Dr Bishop noted that 'there were alien children everywhere, and everybody knew who their fathers were except the children themselves. I was repeatedly asked by the mothers whom these children resembled, and they were evidently very proud to enlighten me.'

Central to their lives were the immemorial rituals of tending the land, and in these remote parts few machines were available to offset the gruelling labour. Haymaking, turf-cutting, potato-picking, sheep-washing and the back-breaking toil of bringing the harvest home, were conducted pretty much as they had been for centuries. Shops were few but a caravan of travelling salesmen would pass through the Dales, staying a few days if necessary to make and mend the men's clothes, or repair the horses' harness. Others would bring fairings, even the latest fashions.

A surprising number of these itinerant traders fell victim to the unpredictable savagery of the Yorkshire weather. Joseph Ford remembers an old man who used to travel the moors selling bottle corks to innkeepers and farmers' wives. One summer day, a skeleton was found in remote Wintergill and, lying nearby, scattered bottle corks. The old man had been overtaken by a snowstorm the previous winter.

The stepping stones at Bolton Abbey

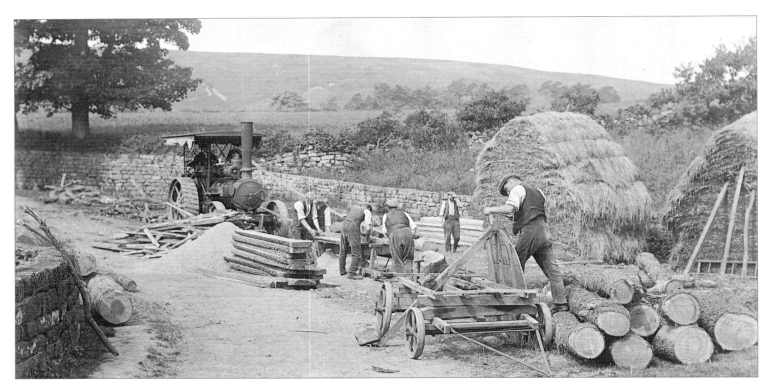

Sawing timber at High Farndale

A TYPICAL YORKSHIRE FARMHOUSE

The slate-flagged farmhouse kitchen in which we sat was part of a building which bore an almost illegible tablet over the door with the date 17—— upon it, the last two figures and the initials of the original owner which accompanied it being erased by time. From the beams hung the bacon and the hams which the dalesman regards as the best sort of decoration for any room – in the days of plenty it was not unusual to find one or two in the best bedroom.

At one side of the kitchen was a huge fireplace kept going with peats and a pile of faggots which never seemed to decline. In front of its blazing heat on the weekly baking day the bread was put to rise covered with coarse white clothes, and into its mighty oven went the bread and the pastries and the oven cakes, which were deliciously 'crunchy' for the first day or so after baking but which by the end of the week needed a good set of teeth to cope with them.

Only a few steps from the kitchen was the icily cold whitewashed dairy, with its stone shelves, its stacks of milk kits and cans, and a slightly sickly atmosphere of much-washed air, a sense of cleanliness that was too scrupulous to be comfortable. Beyond was a lofty room in which the wool was stored after shearing, and an added room full of a mixed cargo of farmer's lumber and domestic odds and ends.

You would have to look long to find the parlour in this house. Indeed, it was not until I found an unexplained window at the side of the house that I knew such a room existed. It was never used save at the time of a funeral or a wedding. Only once in many years did I ever peep into its lace-curtained sanctity to catch a glimpse of an ancient piano, with fretwork front and red-silk folds, a picture – probably 'after Landseer' – of a dog in a kennel, a polished cabinet containing the best tea service, which had doubtless never known the friendly warmth of tea, and a confusion of knick-knacks scattered round the walls. It was the smallest and least comfortable room in the house, and for the most part it was not even regarded as belonging to the place. It was a forgotten room.

Harry J. Scott

GREAT RESPECT FOR EATING AND DRINKING

In the substantial farm houses, eating and drinking were held in great respect. People could neither work nor play if they were poor eaters. Breakfast at seven in summer and eight in winter, dinner at noon, tea or 'drinking' at four, and supper when all work was done, were the usual meal times. When men were working in the fields, their food would be taken out to them, and called 'afternoon drinkings.' In haytime and harvest, a 'forenoon drinking' would be sent into the field about half past ten. The field workers observed a custom, which I think must have come down from very ancient beliefs in the good or evil spirits which watched over the crops. In quaffing a beverage they never drank to the bottom of the pint pot. A little of the drink was always cast upon the ground. May not this have been a survival of the libation to the gods? It was so carefully observed by all that I think it must have had a religious origin. If a man had half a pint of ale standing by his horse he never omitted to cast a small portion on the earth. This was not to clear off a sediment, for there was no sediment. It was like a gift back to the earth.

All meals were substantial. Small French breakfasts or light afternoon teas would have been scorned. Until about 1880 the chief drink was home brewed ale. The first brew was sweet and heavy. It was kept for family use. The second was known as 'small beer' and was produced in quantities for the thirsty workers on the farm. Each brewing produced yeast for baking day, and for giving to cottagers, who did not brew, for their baking. Women were expected to know how to brew, as well as to bake and cook. Gradually the local breweries began to retail supplies of beer to the farms in nine gallon barrels, and they always gave a jug of yeast. A new excise system, about 1880, favoured the big breweries and discouraged home brewing, by requiring an inspector to be notified every time there was going to be a brew.

Abundance, rather than variety, characterised the fare at meal times. Any more than two courses (as we should now say joint, vegetables and sweets) would have been regarded as affectation. But those two courses had some weight in them, and second helpings were welcomed, as a compliment to the cooking. Soups were rarely used, except for invalids, but in substantial form they were served under the name of 'broth' when boiled meats were on the table.

When company were present, a bottle of wine would be placed on the table. Sometimes it was port. More often it was a home-made wine – cowslip, coltsfoot, primrose, blackberry, parsnip, rhubarb, raisin, and others. The very names were poetical and their nature was potent. A light summer drink was nettle beer. A winter pick-me-up was elderberry syrup with hot water and a spoonful of gin. There was sad excess in spirit drinking – chiefly of gin, which was brought from the market

Milkmaid at Low Hawsker Farm

Potato pickers, East Ayton

Ampleforth

town in gallon jars. Whisky came later. To say that spirit drinking worked more havoc in the countryside than anything else, is no teetotal prejudice. It is ghastly fact, as many families knew to their cost. Some market days were a tipsy pandemonium by three o'clock, and many a farmer could not have got home, if his sensible old mare had not known the road there. Nothing is more creditable to the farmers of to-day than their great improvement in sober habits.

Everyone thinks that he knows what Yorkshire pudding is. But the stuff served under that name in some expensive restaurants, is a miserable slab of paste compared with the real thing. It was mixed and well beaten up in a basin, poured into a large square heated pan, partly cooked in the oven first, and then finished off in front of the fire under the roasting joint, where it was soaked in rich hot gravy dripping from the meat. On special occasions, a pound of currants would be stirred into the pudding. It was usually served piping hot, separately before the joint, not along with it.

C.J.F. Atkinson

REPARTEE OF THE FARMHOUSE DINING TABLE

We were always ready for the riddle – and asking riddles was then much on the go – 'What relation is a doormat to the foot-scraper?', the answer to which was: 'a step-father'. Then there was the cow riddle – 'What is it has four stiff standers, four dilly-danders, two lookers, two crookers and a wig-wag?' Year by year the tale was told, and always well received, of the farmer's wife who gave a tramp a good meal on the understanding that he sawed up some wood. When he left the kitchen he made straight off, and the farmer's wife called after him about the logs to saw. He replied: 'I saw 'em as I came in, and I saw 'em as I went out, – good morning!'

Other witty remarks – or *we* thought them so – one heard week by week at farmhouse tables, were: 'Thoo's better ti keep a week nor a fortnight!' 'Them what eats t'most pudding gets t'most meat.' That, of course, meant that if hungry lads were filled with stick-ti-yer-ribs suet – or Yorkshire pudding – they would not have room for much meat.

'Reach to and mak yerselves at home, *I* is and I wish you

all were!' was another remark which always raised a laugh. 'Fingers were made afore forks' was often heard with the apology 'It's mebbe nut very genteel ti pick bones with yer teeth, but gentry losses a lot of sweet meat with their fine manners. Nearer the bone, sweeter the meat.'

'Some lad's bellies is like bottomless-pits, and others has eyes bigger than their bellies – they'll eat till they're brussen and rifting' was a frequent reproof to gluttons and to those who did not 'clean up their troughs'.

I can add another story in the same connection. A yeoman farmer invariably used to say when he sat down as a guest: 'When I gans to anybody else's house I allus eats as mich as ever I can; coz if I'm welcome it pleases 'em; and if I isn't welcome it vexes 'em.'

J. Fairfax-Blakeborough

MINIMAL COST OF LIVING

Very little of the farmer's income was needed for 'the cost of living.' As for clothes, they were of sound durable material, made by local tailors and dressmakers, and lasted for years, first as 'best,' then as 'second best,' and finally, 'to slip on.' A travelling tailor would come and stay at the house for a week, to make and mend men's clothes. His pay was half a crown a day 'and his meat.' A dressmaker would do the same for the women's clothes, but her pay in cash, was only a shilling a day. A journeyman saddler would come once a year and stay three or four days to mend harness. The good folks furnished the house once for all when they were married. Additions were made as the family increased, or as some relative died, and left the fine old family pieces, or linen, to be treasured as heirlooms. But there was no thought of refurnishing. Travel was provided for by a gig and one or two good horses fed – and often bred – on the farm. So there were no 'running expenses.'

C.J.F. Atkinson

'The Road to Lastingham'

The blacksmith at Lealholm Hall Farm, Rosedale

CONDITIONS IN 'T'MEN'S CHAMER'

The sleeping accommodation of the hired lads and farm labourers seventy years or so ago was scanty and would have been thought rough in these days. The old man told me (and I myself remember) that servants ascended a ladder through a manhole to reach what was known as 't'men's chamer' and sometimes only a wood partition with one end open like a stall in a stable, separated them from the maidservants. In the attics there was often no system of ventilation as the square of glass let into the roof for light was not meant to open. The roofs were low and were not underdrawn so that care had to be taken in moving to avoid knocking the head against the heavy oak beams. In thatched roofs and those attics used for storing apples and bacon, rats abounded and held midnight revels. Rats, apples, bacon and general lack of ventilation combined resulted in the attics coming to have a peculiar smell which could not have been healthy especially in view of the fact that the men 'living in' had few opportunities of having a bath and kept all their dirty clothes in their bedroom till such time as their 'weshin' went yam' – possibly once a month.

J. Fairfax-Blakeborough

KEEP THE HORSES WARM

There was a general idea that horses should be kept warm at all costs. It was thought that the horse having sprung from some far-off Eastern country – no one quite knew where but the parts whence the scriptures originated and where it was naturally a very hot climate – they should be in as warm an atmosphere as possible. There was also a belief that it helped to improve their coats and make them glossy if stables were free from draught and as hot as a conservatory. This idea was put into practice by stopping up every ventilation hole with straw and the bottom of the doorways with old sacks or bedding. The old-time stables were often low (owing to the hay-chamber above them) and there were rarely windows in them hence it was possible, especially in winter, when all the horses 'laid in', to get up considerable heat and for the hired men to be more or less comfortable however unhealthy it was for them and the horses. First thing in a morning the air was fit to knock you down and choke you on opening the stable door. It made us gasp and our eyes run with ammonia and one wonders how horses' eyes, feet and lungs stood it.

J. Fairfax-Blakeborough

Staff at Coverdale's cobblers, Pickering

A FILTH-LOVING ANIMAL

There was a general idea in those days that the pig was naturally a dirty and filth-loving animal. That he throve in squalor and dirt and the pigstyes at most farms would now be considered a disgrace. There was often no drainage from them, the floor was earthen, and the piggery received no attention till there was absolutely nothing else to be done about the place. The result was that when at last their turn DID come to be cleaned out it was a longish and far from pleasant job. One stye or more, was often set apart for sows at pigging and a batten of straw was possibly put down for her otherwise little bedding was wasted on the pigs. There were one or two farmers in that day who were great advocates of the open-air system of pig rearing and let them out all day in the paddocks and woodlands when any were near. The surprising fact is that though their pigs did so much better than anyone else's and they were more successful with their litters and had to provide less food for their pigs their example was not more followed. It had been handed down as a tradition with these farmers that when pig-farming was conducted on an extensive scale this open-air treatment was the one resorted to and they used to say: 'You can't beat natur'. They were in the minority, however, for the piggery was the most neglected part of the whole farm sixty years ago

despite the fact that bacon played such an important part in the daily dietary of the house and also, possibly, in the payment in kind of certain obligations to farm hands and others.

C.J.F. Atkinson

AN OCCASION FOR EXTRA HOSPITALITY

A regular occasion for extra baked meats and extra hospitality was the killing of a fat pig. The hams and flitches were carefully cured in the cellar, and then hung up for a year, but all the rest of poor piggie was some form of luxury which had to be enjoyed without delay. Luscious spare-rib, succulent brawn from cheeks or 'chaps,' juicy chine, savoury fry from liver and kidneys, even the 'craps' which were left when the lard had been rendered out of the leaves of internal fat – all were delicacies, to be appreciated only by those who knew. Family and servants enjoyed extras at breakfast and dinner. Relatives and neighbours were invited to join in. Portions were sent as presents to friends, especially to those unfortunate ones who lived in towns and could never kill a pig of their own. In their lives, pigs are about the least attractive of animals, but in their deaths they spread goodwill

Haymaking in Duncombe Park, Helmsley

and radiance far and wide. There was many a blessing on their memory. Nay more, groups of men leaning over the door of a stye, on a Sunday afternoon, and comparing piggie's points, would discuss with watering mouths how sweet his different parts would taste when he had given his last grunt.

C.J.F. Atkinson

''LOWANCES AND DRINKINGS'

I can recollect when we cut all our hay and corn crops with scythes ('lyes' we used to call 'em), and despert back-aching, hard work it was! There were no self-binders when I was a lad, and not many had reapers, so young and old in the villages were engaged by farmers to work in the fields. The bairns made bands, the women tied up sheaves, and some of 'em could stook as well as any man. Often there were twenty or thirty working in one harvest-field in those days – all as merry and happy as could be. Them there self-binders put an end to the army of harvest workers and also put an end to the song, laughter and fun which came from every cornfield. In those times ten-o'clocks and four-o'clocks used to be sent from every farm to the workfolk. These refreshments were called ''lowance', or 'drinkings', and for half-an-hour or so the horses and everyone else, were given a spell whilst the

bread and cheese, the fatty cakes, custards, tea and beer were put out of sight. Every farmer got in a cask or two of beer for hay-time and harvest; but now giving 'lowance seems to have gone out of fashion, like a lot more of the good old customs which made harvest-time so pleasant when the weather let us get on with the job. Before self-binders were invented the machine reapers had put an end to mowing with scythes, but there was still the tying up of sheaves to be done. When the land was mucky there were more thistles than was pleasant for those who had to keep the stookers supplied as they followed on in the procession. They took a pride in setting up their stooks so that they could stand up to a wind, so that they would turn water, and so that they were at just the right angle to catch all the sun to dry them off before leading to the stack. There was always a lot of fun and excitement when the last patch of corn came to be cut, for it was often wick with rabbits and hares which now began to bolt when the standing corn gave less and less cover. The farmer and a friend or two usually had guns – the old muzzle-loaders which had such a kick with them and didn't allow of quick shooting – and the lads and men had sticks. Although a lot of rabbits got away amongst the stooks there was always a fair number to go to market and everyone employed got one or a couple to take home.

J. Fairfax-Blakeborough

Gathering turf at Lastingham

Sheep washing at Kirkham Abbey

ARMSTRONG, THE TURF CUTTER

Armstrong is turf cutting. He is the handy man of the farm and lives at a picturesque thatched cottage near by. He is a genial son of the dale, and is familiar with every nook and cranny in the length and breadth of Bilsdale, and can relate no end of stories touching on the district. He can cut turf, ring a pig, set a mole or a rat trap, beat for game, cut a turf or make a rook, and, in fact, as we have said, turn his hand to anything pertaining to a farm. He is as straight as a poplar, and his long spells of exposure to the open air have bronzed his face to a good standing colour.

To-day the turf is too hard for him to cut such a thickness as he would like. The implement for cutting is similar in shape to a hay spade, though smaller, except that it is turned up about two inches on one side. The spade is six feet in length and has a wooden cross arm at the end for pushing with the hands. The turf cutter fixes round the waist what are called 'Nappers,' a V shaped piece of hard wood, about two inches thick, fastened round the body with strong cord or leather, for protection's sake, as in cutting a turf the whole body is pushed forward with the wooden cross arm of the implement pressing against the 'nappers.' Being desirous of cutting a turf, we fix on the apparatus and cut *one* turf and feel quite satisfied with the effort made. The next business is to 'rook' the turves, otherwise to place them in cocks to dry; under the directions of skipper Armstrong we build a rook and were much gratified on our return visit two months later, to learn that it had not fallen, but had stood intact till harvested.

Michael Heavisides

'TOUSLING' THE SHEEP

In my young days sheep washing was the procedure. A brook was dammed up, forming a pool of about three feet deep, and the sheep were thrown in from a small fold. A farm labourer

or the farmer himself would, after donning an old suit of clothes, stand up in the water and grab the astonished animal and give it a severe 'tousling,' after which it would swim off to a shallow and so reach dry land – wondering no doubt what humans would be up to next.

C.J. Maltby

A NOISY VILLAGE GREEN

I was amused by the complaint of some old ladies who went to stay in a village, one of the charms of which is the spacious green on which stands the village pump, and ancient trees of tremendous girth. The latter have seen many generations of village cricketers come and go, and were doubtless there when there was dancing round the maypole, and other rural sports and exercises now forgotten. Well, the old ladies looked forward to sitting under the shade of those trees, and spending happy, peaceful hours with their books and knitting, undisturbed by any sound but those from the anvil at the nearby smithy, and the rooks in the trees around the church. But morning by morning, the peace was broken, and they were driven away by a series of dog fights. Two dogs met on the green, flew at each other, and before they had really settled down to business, other dogs arrived from all quarters to join in. The sounds of battle, according to the old ladies, were like the cries of a pack of wolves. These battles were too terrifying for them, and they quite changed their opinion of the peace and charm of village greens. These morning dog fights are of such regular occurrence in villages, and in the market-squares at little country towns, that the residents take no notice of them. They are part and parcel of the life of rural England – eternal disputes, which never seem to be satisfactorily settled! It is the terriers and sheepdogs which seem to start the trouble, and although the foxhounds out at walk, a greyhound or two, and dogs the breeding of which is a bit of a mystery, may join in, they merely add to the noise without taking much active

Askern

part. One sometimes wonders how many dogs, and how many different breeds there are in country villages and little market towns . . . As for cats – they are legion!

J. Fairfax-Blakeborough

THE VILLAGE POSTMAN

A village postman once remarked to me: 'I'm nowt but a walking newspaper, or so folks seem to think. Everywhere I goes men in the fields and on the roads expects me to know "the latest". I'll own up I sometimes slips the wrapper off either Robbison's or Charlton's paper – they gets one by post every day, drat 'em! – and just has a squint at the racing and news. You know, one has to be able to say *summat*; that's why I has a glance at owther Robbison's or Charlton's paper – whichever wrapper comes off easiest. I've mentioned to 'em once or twice like, that I've just took the liberty when there's a big race on, or one of these criseses, and they've told me they don't mind. As a matter of fact it was only last week Jack Robbison said to me, "Mather!" he says, "You needn't make no confessions in no way, and you needn't mak no 'pologies, coz we can allus tell when you've had the wrapper off, and we've no objections, coz we knows you must offens cuss at having to come here six days a week sometimes with nowt but the paper, so you're welcome any time you want to have a peep." Of course one has to be very pertickler for you aren't even supposed to read postcards, let alone open anyone's

Feeding the ducks, Ormesby

paper, and I should likely get the sack if it was known I had even so much as a squint, for Post Master Generals and all them there high up chaps in the post office don't know what's expected of us in the country. We've got to be acquented with all the news or else we'd be thought uncivil or unsociable.'

To postmen who have the most isolated rounds to scattered farms and houses, often lying far apart, the members of each family in his area are so well known to him that he addresses them by their christian names. His coming is an event, a break in the monotony of the day, and he is not only as welcome as the gossiping pedlar or ballad monger of yore, but has in a way

Rosedale's one-armed postman at the Lion Inn, High Blakey

succeeded both. He knows the news local and national and, it is therefore not unusual to hear conversation amongst rustics interspersed with ''cordinglie to what the postman said', or (incredulously), 'That'll be one of the postman's tales'. We have known many instances when through illness or some other cause manpower has been short and it has been decided to 'wait while the morning when the postman comes – he'll give us a hand if we catch him afore he gets by'. And so he does, Her Majesty's mail biding till such time as the required help has been rendered. Not only is he the deliverer of letters but out of sheer good nature he also collects to save a long walk to those far distant from the nearest pillar-box. If he has no occasion to call he blows his whistle to announce that he is nearby, and if there are letters to be posted or other urgent commissions for him to carry out, his waited-for signal brings someone to meet him. It is he, more often than anyone else, who puts right stock which have 'gotten wrong', or who reports that sheep or horses have 'brokken lowse', and are straying. Rural postmen it is who have in many cases provided the police with the first information of tragedies, and who have discovered the dead bodies of missing folk, and postmen, too, who can give helpful tips to the gamekeeper, the huntsman, naturalist, mushroom and bramble gatherer, and to those in search of local information, be its character what it may.

J. Fairfax-Blakeborough

CASES OF PRE-NUPTIAL LAXITY

The school-mistress of one village school 'happened a misfortune,' which soon advertised itself, both to the whole village and to the school children. Country children are

Amateur artists at Beauchief Abbey, near Sheffield

astonishingly wide awake on such matters. She had hitherto borne an irreproachable character, and was the victim of a heartless scoundrel. She was more sympathised with than condemned. The school managers came to a deadlock over the question whether she should be dismissed at once with three months' salary, or kept on till her notice expired. Half, including the vicar, were in favour of the former course, while the other half, who were her sympathisers, and also economically inclined, were in favour of the latter. The whole village took sides, with the inevitable 'threeaping and differing.' So obstinate were the managers that a local Solomon was called in to deliver judgment as to who were in the right. He wasted no time in bush-beating, but promptly and very wisely decided that the school was there for the good of the children, and not the school-mistress, and therefore the unfortunate woman must go at once. The vicar's wife who had been the principal stone-thrower, was cleverly rebuked by the great lady of the village for her lack of charity. Miss Frank had a heart of gold, and was, where erring sinners were concerned, full of love and charity. It is not the way of all old maids when their weaker sisters fall.

At a rather crowded afternoon tea-party at the large house, the matter came up for discussion. The vicar's wife having animadverted strongly on village immorality, Miss Frank turned to her and remarked very quietly, 'At the next meeting of your Mothers' Union of which you are so proud, ask Mary Cartman how soon her George was born after the wedding, Susan Blades how soon Susie was born,' and so on, naming at least half a dozen of the mothers and their first-born. It appeared that nearly half of those superior matrons had each a little past of pre-nuptial laxity.

R.W.S. Bishop

AN ALARMING THUNDERSTORM

This alarming thunderstorm in May, 1910, was the worst I ever remember. It occurred at the time of the death of King Edward VIIth. I was 16 years old & lived at Sherburn, E.R. Yorks. The uncurbed flow of water brought chalk from the wolds, & after this alarming flood it could be seen like a winding white river where it lay deposited on the steep hillside fields. Lightning tore open the field shown here.

The three ladies standing by the gap in the hedge are 1. Maud Lawson, 2. Evelyn Lawson, 3. Mrs Fryer — daughters of the neighbouring farmer, John Lawson.

W.P. (Message written on the postcard 'After the Flood' below)

'After the Flood', East Heslerton Grange

Debris from the storm in Ebberston village

Traveller's family at Boroughbridge for the Horse Fair, c. 1896

Chapter 5

'DELIGHTFUL & MOST IMPROVING ENTERTAINMENTS'

*A*uthor of The Wensleydale Hounds, Past and Present, Captain Frederick Chapman was the epitome of the huntin', shootin' and fishin' enthusiast. A crack shot, he represented England in international rifle-shooting competitions and also held the record for the most grouse killed in a single day, 85 brace on Bowes Moor on 12 August 1872. In that season he shot a total of 3,017 grouse, another record but one he had to concede to Earl de Grey who in 1889 bagged no fewer than 3,081.

The Captain prided himself most on his skill as a trout fisherman and 'killed more salmon in one season in the Yore [Ure] than was ever killed before, viz.: sixty-seven fish'. Succeeding his father as Master of the Wensleydale Hounds, he transferred his attentions to the otters of the River Ure. In his zeal to be in the forefront of the chase, his waders often filled with water but the Captain would refuse to stop and dry them out. As a result, he lost the use of both his legs and spent the last twenty-five years of his life in an Eastbourne nursing home.

Edmund Bogg, a Leeds picture-framer, directed his energies in very different directions. He founded the Leeds Savage Club, a curious name for a group of local artists, writers and musicians, but one that allowed Bogg to preside at meetings wearing the headgear of a Red Indian chieftain. Under the leadership of 'T'owd Chief', the Club made frequent excursions into the Dales and Moors and these trips formed the basis for Bogg's many topographical books about the area. His reputation was immediately established with his first book A Thousand Miles in Wharfedale, published in 1892. Like other authors mining this vein, Bogg dutifully rehashes all the hoary old tales of earlier books, but unlike them he includes some vivid descriptions of people he encounters and any unusual incidents that befall him. The extract included in this chapter, 'An Accident under Whernside', gives a dramatic account of a misadventure following a pot-holers' concert party Bogg had arranged in the great cave there.

Pot-holing was still very much a minority interest, but the other pastimes referred to in this chapter – sea and river fishing, horse-racing, the Feasts and Hiring Days – provided a bright foil to the mundane routines of millions of working-class people. And in 1897, of course, there was to be a unique addition to the gaiety of the nation in the form of the Diamond Jubilee Celebrations.

Scarborough beach

ARRANGEMENTS FOR LOCAL REJOICINGS

The members of the Committee which has been appointed to arrange the 'Local Rejoicings' on the 22nd of June, desire to raise a sum of £2000 to meet the needful expenses.

The proposed 'Rejoicings' will be as follows:– (1.) A 'Treat' will be given to all Scholars on the registers of our Day and Sunday Schools. The 'Treat' will consist of a Medal, and a Tea, and, after the Tea, Entertainments in Greenshead Park, and in Longley Hall Park offered for the occasion through the courteous agency of Major Beadon. (2.) There will be a Procession of the Mayor and Corporation, the Volunteers and other Public Bodies through the main streets of the Borough, and a 'sing' of the Scholars in St George's Square – as on the occasion of Her Majesty's Jubilee.

The sum of £2000 is on the estimate of a shilling a head, which will cover the expenses of Medal, Tea and Entertainments for the Scholars, and the necessary outlay on the Poor People's Treat.

Whatever sums may be raised for Trained Nurses for the sick poor, and for the establishment of a Free Library, all are agreed that 'Local Rejoicings' must take the first place. I appeal, on behalf of the Committee, to all classes in the community to give us their generous support. The character of the 'Rejoicings' will to a certain extent, be influenced by the amount raised.

I wish to remind my fellow-townsmen that we are about to commemorate not only an event unique in the history of the English nation, but also to give expression to the loyalty of Huddersfield to an aged monarch who, by her absolute devotion to the best interests of her people, by her sympathy with every form of sorrow and suffering, and by the influence of her character, has won our truest affection and our deepest respect.

May this year, 1897, shine out amongst the brightest annals of the town to which we belong!

James W. Bardsley, Chairman of the Committee for Local Rejoicings, Huddersfield Year Book, *1897*

THE TOUGHEST FOWL IN ENGLAND

Cricket was my favourite pastime in summer, and the only game I saw the local farmers and labourers play was quoits, which was played on a patch of ground adjoining each pub. At the annual feasts, which were held in the Dales in those days, much excitement was worked up at this game, for which a copper kettle was usually the first prize.

Another event at these feasts was a cock-chasing competition, one for juniors and another for seniors. Someone would give us an ancient bird which would be turned loose in a small field. The competitors, with their hands tied behind their backs, would then be released, and the one who caught the bird first with his mouth became the owner. With fifteen to twenty competitors it was astonishing how soon the bird was captured. Whichever way it went it would be quickly headed off and tired out. I recollect one year another boy and I made a dive for the bird as it dashed to a

Men's cycle race, Diamond Jubilee celebrations, Pickering, 1897

The unveiling of Queen Victoria's statue, Sheffield, 4 May 1904

The Carroch family picnicking at Belle Isle Wood, near Leeds

Kilnsey Crag, Coniston

hole in the corner of the field where the water was supposed to go. When we were hauled out by the hind legs the other boy was found to have hold of a mouthful of feathers, but I had a good grip of one of its wings, and was judged the winner. Someone in the crowd offered me a shilling for the cock, but I proudly took it home for my mother. She took three days struggling with this bird, first boiling it, then stewing it, and finally roasting it, but still it remained what must have been the toughest fowl in England at that time.

These feasts led to most furious fights as closing-time drew near. There seemed to be, for some reason or other, considerable rivalry between the farm labourers at our village and those of a village on the other side of the dale. The nearest policeman used to patrol the dale from a centre four miles away, and he made it his business to be present on these occasions. But as ten o'clock drew near he usually silently moved away and was to be seen no more for the rest of the night. Pandemonium shortly broke out, bottles and fists flew in equal proportions, and not until everybody was exhausted did they depart for their respective homes. I suppose these feasts were one way of allowing these men to 'let off steam' after a year of hard, humdrum living.

Other highly diverting items on feast days were 'bun-eating' and 'pipe-smoking.' In the bun-eating competition for boys we sat on a wall and were handed a large dry bun. A basin of black treacle was passed along into which you could dip your bun as often as you liked. The prize went to the lad who consumed his bun first. A whistle was a necessary epilogue. My most vivid memory is of being smeared all over with black treacle, face and clothes alike.

In pipe smoking the men sat on a wall and were given a clay pipe filled with cut-up twist tobacco. At a given signal they all lit up and the prize went to the one who could make the tobacco last the longest without letting it go out. The facial expressions of the competitors as they tried to draw life into a dead wad of tobacco would bring shrieks of delight from the spectators.

C.J. Maltby

GAY DOINGS AT KILNSEY FEAST

Kilnsey Feast is celebrated in Craven. Formerly, great feats of wrestling were performed, the dalespeople being mighty wrestlers. It is worthy of notice that in those English counties where the Celt continued strongly represented, the sport of wrestling flourishes to our own day; and conversely, in those places – minor districts even – where wrestling yet, or until recently, has flourished, the traces of Celtic influence are to be found in all the important topographical features. Here are still gay doings, the country people attending from near and far, racing, jumping, and dancing on the green, the echoes of music and revelry giving back from the walls of the old rock. One race is to the top of the western side of the crag, at the least dangerous place, which puts to the test the breathing powers of the very strongest. It can hardly be described a race – it is merely a creeping up and a scramble down. The writer once joined in this contest and he is not likely to forget his rapid descent down the crag in this race. Starting off with a jump, the flight to the bottom was only a matter of a few moments, luckily escaping with slight injury.

Edmund Bogg

Hiring Fair at Pickering

THE HIRINGS AT PICKERING

Pickering is one of three or four – or perhaps half-a-dozen – small towns lying on the outskirts of the dales where we dalesfolk for generations past have gone sightseeing. At these places special Hirings were held annually, where farmers hired their servants for the ensuing year. That belonged to the business part of the day's outing, but in our grandmother's day 'Punch and Judy' shows and the like played a great part in the day's festivities and attractions. The annual exodus of dalesfolk to one or other of these small towns naturally depended on which lay nearest to the dales from which they poured in large numbers. A hundred years ago it was a great event, but even these old towns themselves are changing. Pickering is not just the same as it was even as I first remember it. The once dimly-lighted shops look brighter with the newly-installed electric light. Now you go to an up-to-date garage to engage your taxi, where once you saw a motley crowd of farmers and their wives with their market baskets selling butter and eggs. The ancient-looking horse-drawn gigs have given place to motor-cars. The 'Punch and Judy' show has gone and in its place is the picture house. The people, too; some of the men seem to persist in growing beards, but the modern Eve has been busy changing the appearance of its population.

Joseph Ford

DISGRACEFUL SCENE AT WHITBY

Four boys named John Howard, William Graham, Thomas Gatenby and William Coopseall were running races in a passage at Haggateshall on the 7th May. They were absolutely naked and causing a gathering of great crowds and therefore an obstruction of the thoroughfare; together with serious damage. Ladies could not pass at the time. The racing on Saturday around 8 o'clock took place before a crowd of about four hundred. The prisoners were fined 10s each or in default to be imprisoned for seven days.

Whitby Observer, *8 May 1870*

MUSIC IN SWALEDALE

A certain writer bemoans a lack of power of musical expression and feeling in the dalesfolk of this and other adjacent places. Experience of 'German bands' or their like in places abroad must have spoilt the ear of this traveller; we, at any rate, cannot honestly concur in his opinion. Every village from Reeth to Keld has its 'band,' the fame of whose attainments has spread far beyond the dales, though, we believe, there are those who detect nothing soul stirring in the skirl of the bagpipes. Apart from this, however, here before us

The sands at Whitby

Muker Brass Band marching to the village's Agricultural Show, 1908

'The brave women of Runswick Bay who launched the lifeboat to save their husbands', 12 April 1901

is a most antiquated and primitive structure and over its lintel writ in large and ancient characters, so that even he who runs may read, the magical words 'BAND ROOM,' probably the smallest and most primitive Hall of Harmony in the kingdom.

As bearing on the notorious love of 'Swardal' folk for their home fastnesses, Richard Kearton, in his fine book, 'With Nature and a Camera', tells how he knew a little girl living high up Swaledale who was compelled to accompany her parents and reside in a Lancashire spinning town. One day some of her relations sent a round of fresh butter to them wrapped up in the cool-keeping leaves of the common Dock, whose large foliage tufts grow in plenty by the stony road and beck-sides from Thwaite to Reeth. 'The little girl's heart,' he writes, 'remained so true to the land of her birth, that she seized one of these (leaves) and cried, "let me kiss it, mother; it has come from dear old Meucar."'

Edmund Bogg

A FISHING EXPEDITION AT RUNSWICK

Runswick is not unlike Staithes, but has the advantage of foliage, which is an additional charm. The bay is glorious, and perfect in form. On the beach we meet an old weather-beaten fisherman who has not taken toll today, so we ask him to pull us out into the bay, and also would like to fish. A little barefoot girl, fleet of foot, slips up to the village to fetch a herring for bait, and returns just when we are ready to push off. The bay is a picture as we cut through the water; then when we are well out, the anchor is dropped to the present delight of the young scion, who is eager to fish. There are two hooks on each line;

these are baited, and as soon as they are some distance down, we can feel the fish at the bait. We draw the line up and two silver whiting reward our pains. After a while the young scion turns pale and retires from the sport, placing himself under the mater's care, for a short time. The fishing, however, goes on briskly, the old fisherman taking the vacated position; and after half-an-hour's exciting fun, we return to land with about seven pounds of fine fish, all whiting. On landing we seek quarters and partake of 'the cup that cheers'; then rested and refreshed, we wend our way to Hinderwell station, as the shadows of evening gather around us. To lovers of nature, this little trip will always prove delightful, as the two fishing villages are full of quaint and picturesque sights.

Michael Heavisides

Rowing party at Burnsall on the River Wharfe

Tennis party, Barmby on the Moor

WHERE WALTONIANS DREAM

So close to the river – which here abounds with grayling and trout – it is no wonder that among anglers Burnsall is a favourite resort. During the season –

> 'Here by the stream,
> Waltonians dream;
> Or ply their craft assiduously,
> With mimic fly,
> Tempt wanton fry,
> And hook them, aye, right-warily.'

The Angling Association, of which Mr J.T. Critchley, of Ilkley, is secretary, preserves a fine length of water, and the fish generally attain a fair size. Day tickets for the privilege of fishing on this particular length are issued by the landlord of the Red Lion Inn.

Who could cross over the bridge without pausing to drink in the quiet beauties around? That footpath running from the steps at the east end of the bridge, leads to the 'Cock'd Hat Close,' and a footpath beyond conducts the visitor to the Skuff, where will be found scarce plants and shrubs which will delight the botanist's heart. This constitutes a most pleasant little walk in itself; for it is nicely secluded, and here and there glimpses can be had of most lovely prospects. There, too, on the village green, stands the Maypole, and its presence recalls to mind the many joyous scenes which were enacted when May-day rejoicings were general throughout the country. In Wharfedale the good old custom seems to have been more rigidly observed than perhaps was the case in any other part, for, from time

immemorial, May-poles have existed at Otley, Burnsall, and Coniston, and even within recent years festivities have been held at those places, attracting thousands of people from the large centres of industry, who might never have previously seen one of these interesting relics of what was once a national observance.

Fred Cobley

AN ACCIDENT UNDER WHERNSIDE

The writer and a party of artists gave a novel concert in this cave, in the autumn of 1891. The pleasure of this adventure was slightly marred by an accident. The company, numbering about thirty-five, started soon after dusk from Kettlewell, provided with candles and magnesium wire. After much fun in wading through torrents and falling over rocks, the party landed safely in the cave, and not one, we should imagine, will soon forget its weird and gloomy depths. Placing the audience in a recess of rocks, the singers climbed the boulders, which rise, in some instances, to the roof of the cave. The magnesium wire did not act well; one moment a brilliant light would illumine the depths of the cavern, then suddenly expire in the most dense darkness. The scene, the hour, the wild grouping of figures on the rocks, the resounding of song, and the music of the instruments along the cavern walls; below, the splashing of the subterraneous stream, bursting from its tomb; the immense assemblage of rocks thrown in utter confusion along the passage of the cave, and the most profound darkness beyond, with the sounds of laughter, the splashing of water and

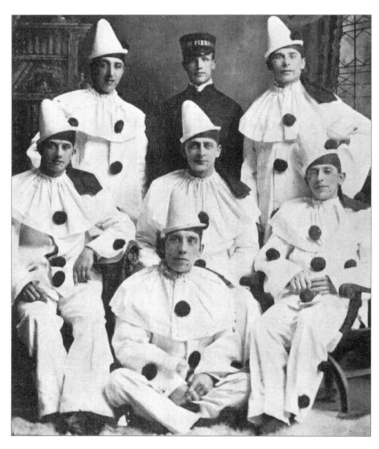

Catlin's pierrots, Withernsea, 1905

the weird strains of music intermingled, formed an impressionist picture, which would rival any scene produced at Drury Lane or Covent Garden. Two of the party, unknown to the rest, with one candle, retired to explore the farthest recesses of the cave, and unfortunately lost their light. In trying to retrace their steps in the darkness, one fell down the rocks, a distance of some twenty feet, into the rivulet, which broke the fall and probably saved his life. The accident, fortunately, happened just at the time when two of the friends, who had discovered their absence, were seeking them, and the rest of the company were leaving the cave for the return journey. Hurrying back along the rocky sides of the cave, with just one solitary candle, whose feeble light made the depths of the awesome cavern more fearful, after scrambling a few hundred yards we paused and shouted, hoping for response; but all was silent save the resounding of our own voices, and the splash, splash of the mysterious rivulet. We were on the point of retracing our steps when the noise of an ominous plunge, as of some heavy body falling into the water, came sounding along the walls, followed by groans and a wild, piercing cry for help. To leap into the stream and scramble along its dark bed was the work of a few moments, which seemed an age, to find the one who had fallen, unconscious in the arms of his friend, who had courageously leapt into the dreary gulf and held him out of the water until assistance arrived. The injured man's face, covered with blood, was bruised beyond recognition. Strange to say, in this hour of need we were deserted by all save the figures in the above engraving, and how our disabled friend was carried through the cave, down the deep glen, and across the steep mountain side, with only the faint light of a candle spluttering in the breeze, I can never understand. The reader will probably say the young man would not be anxious for more cave

adventures. Three weeks later he was well, and, in the company of the writer and two friends, explored another celebrated cave, again under cover of darkness.

Edmund Bogg

NO SITUATION MORE TERRIFYING

I was preparing to mount a big steeplechase horse called Jackdaw Crag to ride a school over fences. A boy held his own horse, Buoyantly, with one hand and tried to give me a leg-up onto Jackdaw Crag with his other hand. Before I was into the saddle Jackdaw Crag reared, then buck jumped, and the big-peaked cap I was wearing came right over my eyes blinding me. I felt with my feet for the stirrup irons and got one in but by this time Jackdaw Crag had bolted. I could not see and the next thing I knew was that he was in the air. I thought he had made another buck till he pecked and I found myself on the ground at the edge of a dry ditch – 'the open grave,' as steeplechase jockeys call it!

Away went Jackdaw Crag with me hung up in the one stirrup. He kicked at me as he galloped and landed one or two well-aimed shots in my ribs. It is said of one knight of yore who had a bad fall of this sort, 'Between the stirrup and the ground, he mercy sought and mercy found.'

Well, I never was so afraid in my life. Bruised and battered, I was clattered along the ground – fortunately it was the thick turf for which Hambleton has long been famous – kicked at and entirely helpless. Certainly I put in a few quick 'Hail Mary's' that the stirrup leather would break. I knew that was my only chance, as those who see a man being dragged are

Stable lads at Mr Dobson Peacock's Manor House Stables, Middleham, c. 1898

absolutely helpless. If they gallop after a horse which is dragging someone they only make him increase his pace. If they try to turn him the odds are they will send the unfortunate victim under the legs of the excited animal, which probably does not understand what it is he is trailing by his side. I know of no situation more terrifying, and none in which spectators are more anxious to do something, yet quite unable. I quite expected that my number was up and that I should soon land a mangled mass. I would not like to live those dreadful seconds again. I was a youth then, and thought little of falls. Indeed, sometimes I rode for a fall, courting and expecting it. To be dragged, however, is another matter. The bravest man in the world trembles at the thought of that and prays he may be freed from such an experience. Had I been on a hard road I should probably have been soon unconscious but as it was I saw those long legs of Jackdaw Crag's going faster and faster. I saw his polished shoes as they were lifted and as they struck at me in an attempt to get rid of the burden the horse had attached to him. He wasn't nearly as anxious to be free from me as I was to be free from him. At last the stirrup leather was torn from the saddle and I lay on the ground with the sky spinning like a roundabout at a fair. I was quite sure that I hadn't a whole bone left in my body, that I should be weeks and weeks in hospital and, worse than all, that I should possibly never ride again.

Despite his mad gallop through the thickly-planted wood and down the road there was not a scratch on the horse, and he was none the worse. As for myself, a doctor from Oswaldkirk was sent for and found I had a dislocated ankle, a cracked rib or two, and a good many black, blue and purple bruises.

J. Fairfax-Blakeborough

TRICKS OF THE TURF

When I was young there were much stranger things done on the Turf than could be accomplished these days. Stewards are much more vigilant and knowledgeable. In 1908 I remember a Malton owner running a horse at Thirsk in a race which looked a gift for him. He was made favourite, but the owner backed the ultimate winner. He had a jockey who 'was paid and did as he was told.' His instructions were to get well away, make the running, and then pull up and dismount a couple of furlongs from home. At the spot indicated the horse pulled up, the jockey dismounted, and the owner, who was standing conveniently near, rushed on to the course. Covered by the jockey he produced from a warm inside pocket a bottle, and with his handkerchief smeared the horse's nostrils with the blood he had that morning collected from a Malton slaughterhouse. Together jockey and owner led the horse back to the paddock with blood trickling from its nostrils and the gory handkerchief much displayed. It was obvious for everyone to THINK that this was a bad case of blood-vessel breaking. The following week the same horse ran at another Yorkshire meeting but no one except the owner dare take the long odds offered. He won and there was no summons to the stewards room afterwards.

J. Fairfax-Blakeborough

ATTACKED BY AN OTTER

Old Tom Jackson, of West Witton, was very keen on otter hunting. He used to walk down to the river two or three

Captain Chapman's otter hounds at Kirkbymoorside

Hull Fair, 1904

times every week in the summer to see whether an otter had passed. There was a bed of sand at Beals Dub which an otter never passed without calling at. Whenever one had passed up or down, he used to send a message up to Thornton by the mail cart which then ran through the Dale.

Next morning my father would leave early with what hounds he could gather together. Tom also started off early the same morning, and they invariably met somewhere between Aysgarth and Redmire Falls.

In my very earliest days, my father used to carry an otter spear, and so did old Tom.

Well, on the occasion alluded to, they had not quite met; but Tom, hearing, and seeing the hounds in full cry below Froddle Dub, got into the middle of the stream at the head of Flesh Dub. As the otter was passing him, he took the liberty of putting his spear into the otter's flank. The otter at once retaliated by seizing Tom by the leg, in which he made his teeth meet, and took a piece clean out of his trousers as big as a five shilling piece. Tom, hallooing as loud as he could, 'Be quick; be quick! he's worrying me,' stuck to the otter; and the otter stuck to Tom, until the hounds came up, when Mr Otter quickly let go and was soon dispatched. This proved to be a very large dog otter. For a long time afterwards, Tom was proud of showing his leg, as well as his trousers.

Captain F. Chapman

CHOPPED BY THE HOUNDS

The longest otter hunt I ever witnessed was with the late Mr Gallon's hounds.

We bolted an otter on the Batts Island, below Cover Bridge.

He took straight up stream, over the Dam stakes, into the deep pool above Ulshaw Bridge, and there he defied us for nine hours. There were a great number of strong roots at very short distances apart. The otter kept moving backwards and forwards from one to another the whole of the time, and we really were no nearer a kill at the end than when we started. I was so stiff with wading, and the hounds so done up with swimming, that, with the greatest difficulty, I persuaded Mr Gallon to call hounds off. We walked across to Cover Bridge Inn, put the hounds up in a very thick bed of straw, had two fires lighted on the Dam stakes to prevent the otter going down stream, and went to bed about eight o'clock, well tired.

We started next morning at five o'clock, up stream. Never had a chirp of music until opposite the west end of Middleham, where a boat used to be kept.

A short distance above Middleham Bridge the hounds marked at a long drain. Mr Gallon's two terriers bolted an otter into a sack which was held over the mouth of the drain. He was carried over the fields and turned into a small pool below Wensley Bridge, where he, unfortunately, got into shallow water, and the hounds chopped him. I heard many people present remark, 'Oh! what murder.' I wonder what any one of them would have done in the position of Master of otter hounds, which had such a stiff nine hours only the day before. Surely the hounds deserved blood. These growlers had not been out the first day, so were evidently disappointed with so short a hunt – 'Blithering donkeys,' I style them. Had the otter gone down stream instead of up, he might have gone into Dyehouse Dub, a long and strong pool, and given another long hunt. But accidents will happen even in the best regulated packs of otter hounds.

Captain F. Chapman

The Meet at Helmsley, c. 1904

QUITE IMPERVIOUS TO WET

Mr John Chapman was Master of the Wensleydale hounds for over forty years. He was, perhaps, best known as 'Old Squire Chapman,' although he never liked being addressed as Squire. He used to say, Esquire belonged to the tail of our aristocracy; that he was a British yeoman who owned sufficient property to enable him to live comfortably and within his income. He was an extraordinary man in many ways. After wading whilst otter hunting all day he would never change his clothes. Frequently when he had not found his otter, or had been defeated by him, he would stay all night at some gentleman farmer's house not far from the river, so that he might have an early start next day. The late Mr Fryer of Fleets, near Cover Bridge, told me that on one occasion when spending the night there he would not have any change of clothing although wet up to the waist. During the night the maid had dried his shoes. Early next morning his first enquiry was for a water trough. Being told of one, he walked out in his stockings and at once put his shoes into it, adding, 'How could I put on such nasty hard things, besides, they would be quite wet in less than five minutes after getting to the river side.' If he had an attack of lumbago, which was very rare, he would go down to the river and wade up and down up to his middle for about twenty minutes. This, he said, always did him good. Others tried it but it nearly finished them. I recollect when he was eighty-two years of age, a relative and I got thoroughly wet through whilst trout fishing, and on going up to Thornton for a change, I saw my father sitting quite comfortably in his armchair with quite a little pool

of water on the carpet at his feet. On remarking, 'Pray what have you been doing?' he replied, 'Ah! yes, I forgot, I went out during that heavy shower to sit in the garden chair. It does me good to get well soaked, and softens my old skin.' I immediately got his coat off, and whilst fetching him a dry one, he remarked to my relative: 'As soon as Frank's gone out I'll have that coat on again.' Strange as it may appear, I never remember it giving him a cold or doing any harm. He seemed to be quite impervious to wet.

Captain F. Chapman

NOTED FOR HAVING A WIDE THROAT

It was on the 12th of August when Mr Robinson accompanied by Mr John Booth, of Killerby (father of the late John Booth who was master of the Bedale hounds), were out grouse shooting on Woodale Moor. Whilst having luncheon on the top of the moor, near a spring of water, Mr Robinson grabbed a little moor mouse, which he squeezed to death, and then said to Mr Booth 'I'll bet you five shillings I make Matt swallow this.'

'What,' replied Mr Booth; 'raw, as it is?'

'Yes!' said Mr Robinson.

The bet was accepted. Mr Robinson then rolled the mouse up in a piece of luncheon paper, and put it into his pocket. In the evening, on approaching the village inn, where they usually stayed over night, they found Matt just outside awaiting their return. Matt was a thirsty man, noted for having a wide throat. He saluted the sportsmen with his usual –

'Good evening, gentlemen! I hope you have had good sport.'

'Thanks, Matt,' replied Mr Robinson, 'pretty fair;' and then added, 'I have just made a bet with Mr Booth for half-a-crown, that you can swallow a quart of ale without taking the jug from your lips. If you can do this, I will give you the half-crown, as well as the ale.'

'That's just what I should like,' said Matt. 'You can consider your bet won.'

Mr Robinson ordered the landlord to draw a quart of ale, put it into a brown jug, and froth it up well. He then turned to Mr Booth, to let him see the mouse put into it, and then handed it to Matt, remarking: 'Now, Matt, don't forget, you have to finish it before you take it from your mouth.'

He did so; and when Mr Booth asked if he had tasted anything wrong, Matt said, 'Nay! I didn't 'xactly taste ow't wrong, but I thow't ther' was a bit ov a *hop* in 't.'

Captain F. Chapman

DRAWING OUT A FOX BY ONE'S FINGER

Jammie Holmes at once doffed his coat, turned his shirt sleeve up, and plunging his arm into the hole, drew out the fox, but not before Reynard had got a fang through one of Jammie's fingers. Several of the ladies who were there, on seeing the blood on his hand, uttered exclamations of pity for the poor huntsman. My father at once seized the opportunity of having a 'cap' for him, and in a very few minutes several pounds were subscribed. Jammie being a thirsty man, soon made tracks for the nearest public house, where, after the usual lubricating process, he sang several hunting songs, and remarked, 'I wouldn't mind how often I was bitten at that price.'

On another occasion, I recollect, we ran a fox to ground at Woodhall, in a very long drain, and when the terrier had driven him to the far end, we had great difficulty in getting at him, but Jammie again came to our aid, saying 'I think I can touch him,' and by giving the fox his finger, as before described, drew him out. An old gentleman being close at hand, seeing the blood, at once exclaimed, 'Oh! Jammie, wait a minute till I get a little rum or brandy to put on it.' So he did, to Jammie's delight, for after bathing the wound, he caused great laughter by saying, 'I think I'll try a drop inside, as well.'

Captain F. Chapman

A DISAPPOINTING SPORTS DAY

The weather, which we gather from our contemporaries, spoilt all School Sports held at the end of last term, was not propitiated by the postponement to this term which it forced

Preparing for the 100-yard sprint, Ebberston School Sports Day

Sports Day at Lady Lumley Grammar School, Pickering, July 1910

on us, but when the adjourned date came round on May 9th, treated us most villanously to a day of gloomy coldness, terminating with drizzle, sandwiched in between days wholly worthy of the month of May.

To add to this ill luck, influenza had been busy during the holidays following its usual place of victimising the most valuable persons, and it left Class A so short of competitors, that many events which had promised a keen contest were little better than walk-overs, and the results hardly worthy of Class B.

The arrangements of the Committee to make the best of our decidedly uneven cricket field were excellent, and no hitch occurred to damp the ardour of those spectators and competitors who were able to be present. The handicapping produced exciting races in every case, indeed the *running* in each class was good though no times were taken except for the 100 Yards A, when we find Huddlestone's 11⅗ seconds is at least an average performance. Besides Huddlestone, Brown, Bottomley, Priestley, J.A. Walker and Wall shewed remarkably good form in their running; and Benskin's wonderfully plucky run in the mile, richly deserved the first prize which Huddlestone resigned to him.

The Sack Race was amusing as usual, though. J.A. Walker got his toes into the corners of his sack and, followed pretty closely by his brother, ran away easily from his floundering companions.

The impromptu handicapping for the Old Boys' Race gave it easily to Mr Bradley, who was allowed a considerable start though he turned out to be a first rate runner whose name is not unknown in champion competitions. Mr P. Rittener, starting from scratch, gained on him and made a good second.

The High Jumps, except in Class D, were poor, but in Class A only two competitors out of the seven who entered were able to contest the event, and the winner only jumped 4ft. 2in., much less than he had cleared in practice.

The Long Jumps were spoilt by faulty taking off. The best jumps in Class A (passing the winning distance by nearly a foot) had to be disqualified, and 16ft. 2in. took first prize.

The Cricket Ball throw was most disappointing, 68 yards being far below the true form of the 1st Eleven men; but Brown's Lacrosse throw of 92 yards was distinctly creditable.

Mrs C.E. Freeman distributed the Prizes in a most kind and genial manner and the boys tried to shew how much they appreciated it by the three hearty cheers they gave for her after a few brief words of thanks from the Head Master. Cheers were also given for The Ladies, Mr & Mrs Symons and The Old Boys.

Huddersfield College Magazine, *July 1891*

Chapter 6

WORTHY OF THEIR HIRE

I *only recently discovered that, one hundred years ago, the task Yorkshire's agricultural workers loathed most was not the back-breaking labour of potato-picking, nor even mucking out pig-sties left unattended for months because most farmers believed that pigs thrived on filth. What they hated most was spreading soot. Soot was, indeed is, a highly effective fertiliser. It is also, as M.C.F. Morris points out in the extract from his* The British Workman, Past & Present *included in this chapter, 'Very adhesive when it comes into contact with human flesh'.*

As a result, during the three or more days of soot-spreading, the farm-workers had to be sequestered in their own 'Black Hole'. However, the eventual cleansing operation as Morris describes it here must have been something of a compensation.

This kind of work was certainly unpleasant, but at least it wasn't life-threatening. Hundreds of thousands of Yorkshire's miners, mill-workers and fishermen from its East Coast ports faced daily a very real danger of injury, mutilation or death. And it's difficult to imagine a more hazardous occupation than the one witnessed by Arthur Norway on the cliffs around Flamborough Head. Relying only on a rope, a couple of pulley spikes and the strength of his three colleagues, the collector of gulls' eggs dropped down the cliff face gathering the gleaming blue eggs as he went. Regaining the top of the cliff with the eggs intact was even more perilous.

Elsewhere across the county, many traditional skills were being undermined. The cotton mills of the West Riding were threatened by cheap imports from the USA and the Far East, and the first motor cars would prove a grim portent for many a village farrier and harness maker. Another casualty of the past hundred years is mining for jet. In the 1880s this lustrous black stone enjoyed a tremendous vogue, a fashion led by the royal family who considered it one of the few adornments permissible during the frequent and lengthy periods of court mourning. For several decades, jet brought considerable prosperity to Whitby but by 1914 workable deposits of the stone were virtually exhausted and a new generation shunned its gloomy association with death.

In the nature of things, few workingmen at that time recorded their own experiences. One lively exception is Harry Fletcher who worked as a barge-boy on the rivers and canals of the East Riding and from whose autobiography A Life on the Humber *several extracts are included in this chapter.*

Off-loading brandy at Scarborough

STARTING WORK AT 9½ YEARS OLD

I begun to work for my Aunt Alice, when I was nine and a half years of age. She and her husband were hand-loom weavers, having a large weaving chamber holding two hand-looms – broad hand-looms – a hand bobbin winding wheel and a healding frame. There were also two beds in the chamber in addition. She was a good soul. My uncle was one of the old stock who loved his glass of whiskey, but who enjoyed it by his own fireside and occasionally he would become a bit cranky or merry, by having a whiskey or two, too many. My job was to reach the threads in when my aunt was healding the warp ready for it being woven. It was an easy job but a bit boring, especially on a hot summer's day, and a lad of nine was liable to get drowsy. When that happened a tap on the shins from her foot would be the awakener. My first wage for a full day's labour was threepence for my mother, a halfpenny for myself, and a new-baked, currant tea cake to eat on my way home. Wasn't I 'chuff' when I could swank home with a bit of wage! The pocket money was welcome, for in a country village a half-penny to spend was a mint of money to a lad of nine in those days.

Ben Turner

MESSRS MARSHALL'S WONDERFUL FLAX-MILL

As Kirkstall is the chief ancient feature in Leeds, so the mills are its crowning modern interest. It is difficult to get permission to see one of these, but through the extreme kindness of the Messrs Marshall we had the privilege of seeing their wonderful flax-mill. It is in the part of Leeds called Holbeck, and is a massive building in the Egyptian style, covering an area of two acres. The work is carried on in one huge room, which a partition divides into two, and when Mr Marshall took us in the effect was electrifying. Each frame and each worker standing before it seemed a part of one immense machine which would go on in the same perfect precision and cleanliness for ever, – the workers silent as the grave, – while the resistless chorus of whirrs seemed to fill every chink in the vast place. This vast chamber contains no less than sixty-six sky-lights for the admission of air and light. A series of arches rests on cast-iron pillars, and the air and light thus obtained obviate all the stuffiness of atmosphere one associates with the idea of a mill; the women look healthy and happy, never leaving off work, but seeming to follow it with interest as well as industry. Mr Marshall explained to us in a very lucid way the process through which the flax passes from its pristine state to the finest sewing thread, and he illustrated his explanation by taking us from frame to frame and showing us how the flax

The weaving room at Glover Bros, Wortley Low Mills, Leeds

– guided by the women's skilful fingers, and moved by the resistless force of the huge steam-engine which, like some Hydra, seems omnipresent in the vast chamber – not only gradually becomes soft and fine like flour passing through different mills, but – as it also passes through chemical preparations, it goes through many grades of colour and is finally bleached to snowy whiteness.

In another huge room we found the weavers creating out of the prepared flax coarse towelling, blinds of varied stripes and patterns, every imaginable sort of linen fabric from coarse to the finest. It was very interesting to watch the manufacture of the striped goods, to see the regular dexterity needed in placing the required portions, and in all cases the flight of the little shuttle from side to side bearing the weft across and between the strands of warp. So interesting was it that, spite of the deafening noise which seemed to set all one's nerves loose at once, we were unwilling to leave off looking. After this we went up on the roof, where we saw that the sky-lights rose about nine feet above it, the spaces between being filled with coal-tar and soil to secure an equality of temperature below.

If mill hands are as well cared for everywhere as they are in this wonderful flax-mill they are well off. The women looked well fed and well clothed, and much more civilised than the mill hands we remember to have seen at Birmingham some time ago. Messrs Marshall have built a church, St John's, Holbeck, for the work-people, and seem to care for them in every way. I suppose habit accustoms the hands to the incessant whirr of the steam-engines; there can certainly be little danger that they should waste their time in talk, for hearing is difficult without some effort.

Thomas and Katherine McQuaid

PIECENER IN A MULEGATE

From village life to town life is a great change – I had never been on a train before I was thirteen. I had been to Huddersfield once in a waggon one Whit-Tuesday to a Band of Hope gathering. It was therefore a new adventure for me to go from a little place of one hundred folks to a big place with thousands.

My brother and myself were lucky enough to find a new place to work at. He began work at twelve shillings and I at nine shillings per week. This was a big increase on the nine shillings and five shillings we had been getting before. My father had also got a good place to work at, and if it hadn't been for the shop book debts, etc., we might have been fairly well to do as a working-class household. I was fortunate to become a piecener in a woollen mulegate, and whilst the head spinner and his sons were mighty keen at their job, they were good workers, and the material being good to spin, it wasn't any harder than the job I had left.

Here I got my first dash of vegetarianism. One of the foreman's sons – a young fellow about three years or so older than I – led me to try to be a vegetarian. It lasted with me six weeks, for as a growing lad I was running about a mulegate for ten and a half hours a day. The rice pudding I tried to make do

The rolling frames room, Kaye & Stewart's Broadfield Mills, Lockwood, Huddersfield

for my midday meal was done by three o'clock, and I became as hungry as a hunter by that time, so I gave it up. It was harder to be a vegetarian then than now, for there were not the fancy dishes and different sorts of foods there are to-day. A worker's usual meals were, for breakfast, bread and drip or bread and butter, or a big currant tea-cake or a big carraway seed cake. They were none of your puny little cakes of to-day, but big round things that were home-baked, and many a time in later days I did two of them to my breakfast. The baking day at home was always Thursday. It is a regular day in Yorkshire and at our house yet, and my mother, in those times, used to bake three stones of bread to last the week. Fancy cakes and dainties were not needed; the home-baked bread was good enough. Bacon and eggs, etc., were not common. If we had an egg, it was to our Sunday breakfast. In summer, we might take spring onions, or some lettuce or other greens like watercress, but generally nothing but bread and tea or coffee.

For dinner-time – the midday meal – we would have, on a Monday, a bit of cold meat; on Tuesday a hash, on Wednesday a potato pie, on Thursday some fry and onions, on Friday a bit of potted meat, on Saturday a bit of sausage, and on Sunday the usual joint, always providing the funds ran to it.

For our teas it was again bread and drip or bread and butter, or sometimes a Spanish onion or some 'craps' (pork fat made crisp), and on Sunday teatime, a bit of special home-made cake to make the distinction from the other days. At the worst times our cut of beef was brisket because it went the farthest, and made the most 'drip,' besides being the cheapest cut.

Ben Turner

Slingsby's Band of Hope summer excursion

MOST HEART-BREAKING EXPERIENCE IN THE WORLD

During my latter days at Huddersfield I fell out of work. My loom was pulled down.

If my reader has never been out of work let him be thankful. It is the most heart breaking experience in the world for a man or a woman to have to travel from one mill to another asking a brother man for leave to work. It was the hardest nine weeks I ever had. We had two little children under two years old and nothing saved. My union paid me 7s a week victimisation pay and with the exception of 5s I borrowed from a friend we pulled through but I was never much of a person to sit doing nothing. I must be reading, writing or doing something, and when I was younger it was the same; besides, when trade was slack and times were poor I had to do something. Therefore I bought some cheap fents (short lengths of drapery), and garments, on the hire-purchase system, and set out round the country to sell them in the same way.

I got customers. There was no difficulty there, but the job was getting the money. A few paid up regularly each week, but the majority of them I divided into two classes – those who could, but wouldn't, and those who would, but couldn't pay.

Ben Turner

A DESPERATE YOUTH

I knew of one boy who was very anxious to become a 'full-timer.' What his reason was for wishing to give up school, and work full time at the mill, I do not remember. It was

Bradford unemployed camp at Manningham, Bradford, 1906

Corporation Street, Middlesbrough

almost certainly due to one or other of two causes. He may have hated lessons even for half the day, and have desired to be altogether quit of them, or he may have desired to work full time, and so be able to do more towards the support of his mother. Anyhow, he was in desperate earnest to become a 'full-timer.' When the doctor paid his next visit to the mill, he presented himself, and made application to be allowed to work full time, and insisted that he was of full age to do this. The doctor examined his mouth, and, touching a certain tooth, said, 'I can't pass you as long as you have that tooth in your head.' The boy went out and got hold of a stone in the mill yard, and dashed the tooth out. He then re-presented himself before the doctor, and to his great delight was passed as a full-timer.

William E. Anderton

UNIQUE BEAUTY OF THE YORKSHIRE MILLS

Although only twelve, I had vivid memories of the unique Northern beauty of the mills in winter. No dirt or smoke, only light. I wondered, every time I saw this spectacle, just how many people were busy behind those windows, which threw out gleams that made the wet pavements glisten, and the streets friendly.

On cold rainy nights, the mills looked anything but 'dark and Satanic.' There was a warmth and a proud challenge in the solid mass of light which suggested an activity that went on without supervision, and in all weathers. It was something I never took for granted; I used to stand and feel an admiration for the people who kept the mills going, and I longed to be in there with them!

Wilfred Pickles

WAGES SHOULD BE PAID IN SILVER

The wages at the ironworks are paid on a Friday. From Friday until Monday it constantly happens that the man is half incapacitated by drink. However good his resolutions, he is accosted on his way on pay-day by one tempting possibility after another. One of these possibilities, at any rate, seems to be very difficult to avoid. The wages, for convenience of handling, are paid as far as is possible in gold, an inconvenient form of currency with which to meet the daily expenses of the workman. If the pay-clerk has to give a sum of 30s to 35s, he will pay the 30s with a sovereign and a half-sovereign and the odd shillings only in silver. The workman will therefore have to change his gold coin or coins for silver; and for this purpose the public-house, which takes care to be well

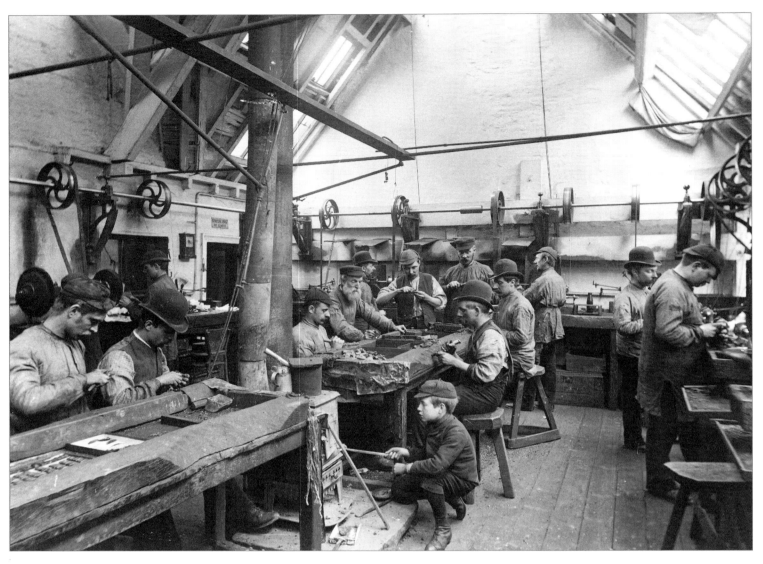

William Wright's jet works, Haggersgate, Whitby, c. 1890.

provided with change at the end of the week, is the most obvious place. It is not surprising that some of the handful of change given to the workman by the publican should, partly in return for these kind offices, be expended on the premises. If the weekly wages could conceivably be paid in silver instead of gold, so that the workman had not a justifiable reason for entering the public-house on his way home, there might be a good deal less intemperance in the town.

In some of the lower quarters there are touts employed by the publicans, who are given drink for nothing if they bring in a customer, and who stand on the pavement and ply the workman with offers of drink. One man, who had to pass five public-houses on his way home from his work, told a visitor that he had to make a separate effort at each one; he had succeeded one winter's afternoon in passing four, and if the fifth had not been there he 'would have got home all right,' but at that last one he succumbed and went in, cold, wet, and tired, to sit in the warm and cheerful room, with the incidental subsequent result that may be imagined.

Lady Bell

FORTUNES OF THE JET MINER

The fortune of the jet miner was as uncertain as the fortune of the whist player when lifting his hand of cards. It had been known for a small group of men to work for weeks, months even, until their small stock of money was exhausted, without ever finding an ounce of the valuable jet; then, in their despair, their fortune might suddenly change, a lucky seam be struck, and they would be doubly repaid for all their labour, if not for all their bitter disappointments. Other small groups of jet miners were known to pool their resources in money and lose every penny of it, never finding jet in sufficient quantities to make a living for themselves. These were obliged to give up and were glad to find employment working for others by the day. Yet some were lucky enough to make fortunes out of the hazardous undertaking.

Although the jet miners of our dales knew just where and at what levels in the shale it might be expected to find the jet seams, yet even with this expert knowledge their mining was nothing more or less than a game of chance. This is easily realised when we consider that jet is only to be found in comparatively small quantities, and the seams, unlike deposits of Limestone, coal or iron, are not continuous; that is to say they do not cover large areas.

Joseph Ford

JET IN GENERAL FAVOUR

Jet seems to be in general favour, for nearly all the newest trimmings show jet in combination with silk etc. for the design is not entirely worked out in jet. So much of this jet trimming is used in Paris at the moment that the makers are unable to obtain skilled hands to execute the orders. Up till quite recently jet has been regarded as exclusively for mourning wear, but, for some time past, we have been wearing beautiful cut buttons of jet, glimmering black tiaras with flashing facets, cameos for the hair, ear-rings and various other personal ornaments all made of glittering black jet, curiously carved in many cases, and perfectly plain and unpolished in others. This season sees the introduction of jet on the evening gowns in embroidered heavy fringes; and in some cases the whole gown is made of jet in an all-over effect in black net over soft green satin. The corsage is sometimes of solid jet embroideries intermixed with silk. Jet and gold, jet and silver, jet and steel, jet and crystal; all are represented and the superb designs in colour show touches of jet introduced into the design. Openwork or net foundations formed of tiny jet bugles strung together or used in wide bands are supplied for coloured evening gowns with good effect. Even the severely tailored gown has buttons carved in jet in small and large sizes and huge jet buckles are appearing on the autumn hats, on the waist-belts and as clasps on opera cloaks, and evening wraps.

Whitby Gazette, *September 1909*

ROYAL PATRONAGE OF WHITBY JET

That the wearing of Whitby Jet ornaments by the lady members of the Royal Family is still a feature of their admiration for what is beautiful and artistic was shown a few days ago by HRH the Princess Victoria (daughter of Edward VIIth) making a visit to and purchasing goods from our late townsman Mr F.R. Winterburn who has an establishment devoted entirely to the business at Harrogate. It is said that the 'course of the waters' at Harrogate and the pure Yorkshire air have been most beneficial to Her Royal Highness who was accompanied by the Grand Duchess Mikhailovitch of Russia and several other princesses and members of Royal Families and it is whispered other members of our own Royal Family may not be entirely unexpected visitors. The few remaining jet workers of the old school will be pleased to hear of the continued patronage given to the trade by one of its oldest representatives whose jet shop in Silver Street was unfortunately burnt out in 1880. It is now more than sixty seven years since Mr Winterburn became first acquainted with the works of the jet shop. They will call to mind the prosperous days when Queen Victoria,

The Old Sulphur Well, Harrogate

grandmother to the present Princess, was the great admirer and patroness of 'real Whitby Jet' and though the days of great productions may never return, there would be ample room for the development of higher artistic taste and a fair livelihood for a number of the descendants of the old trade which, more than any other, will always be coupled with the name of Whitby.

Whitby Gazette, *19 August 1910*

OPENING OF THE NEW CASH RAILWAY

Opening of a Railway by the Mayor of Middlesbro'

At 10.30 this (Saturday) morning the Mayor of Middlesbrough (Mr Amos Hinton) opened the Cash Railway at Messrs John Hedley & Co's. noted drapery establishment, Linthorpe-road, Middlesbrough. The Mayor's daughter was the first purchaser, and the money and check was despatched to the cash desk, and returned with the change in a very short time, and was handed to Miss Hinton amid loud cheers from the large company assembled.

The Mayor said, Messrs Hedley and Co. have this morning introduced to the Middlesbrough public one of the most ingenious contrivances that it had been his pleasure to witness, and which was called a Cash Railway. The Cash received from the customer was put into one of the balls, which was then closed up and sent along the rails to the cashier who does the needful, and places the change in the ball and it comes back to the assistant where it started from. The advantages they would at once see, was that the assistant had no reason to leave the customer, but could remain at his post the whole time and was not kept running about, and spending the time which could be better occupied by persuading a lady to buy something that she really did not want.

Cashier's office, the Co-operative Store, Hull

The Mayor now said we have made a small purchase, and on the check being made out, he despatched it on its journey, and soon received it back with the change. He then said that having set the money ball rolling, he hoped it would roll merrily all through the year, not only in that establishment, but in every tradesman's in Middlesbrough and throughout the country. (Loud cheers.)

Mr Alderman HEDLEY, JP, senior partner, rose and said it was his pleasing and agreeable duty to move a vote of thanks to the Mayor and his daughter for coming to open their New Cash Railway. They were permitted to live in an age of progress. When he was a young man the ladies were willing and agreeable to wait their turn, particularly if they could be served by a good looking, amiable young man like himself. (Cheers and laughter.)

As soon as the formalities were over a brisk business was done by the large company who had assembled to witness the ceremony, and we should imagine that the first day's receipts on the new local railway will amount to a good average per mile.

Middlesbrough Daily Exchange, *3 March 1887*

SLEEPING IN A SOOT CHAMBER

The value of soot as a fertilizer of the soil has long been appreciated, though its use in bygone years was much more general on the Wold farms than it appears to be at the present day; in fact, its use now has wellnigh vanished, the reason being, not that soot has lost its value as a fertilizer, but because the men cannot be induced to handle it.

It may well be imagined that the spreading of soot upon the land, seeing that the work had to be done by hand, was one of the most unpleasant jobs that fell to the lot of the farm men, for soot is apt to be very adhesive when it comes in contact with human flesh. Nevertheless, this dirty work was not without its amusing side. Of course special preparations had to be made for the work, which at Danesdale was carried on extensively. One year no less than five hundred quarters of soot were spread over a hundred acres of land, for which the weather conditions had to be favourable.

It was obviously impossible for the men to be dressed in their ordinary garb in the performance of this work; no suit of clothes could possibly stand such an ordeal, and no amount of brushing and washing could restore them quite to their

Packing the day's catch, Scarborough

original state. Moreover, it took several days to complete the task. Where, then, it may be asked, were the men to sleep? Of necessity their ordinary beds, as well as their ordinary garments, had to be discarded. What was to be done? Sleep they must have, and they could not repose in the open fields, for it was then winter. And so the only thing to be done was to provide a special soot chamber for the men to sleep in, which might be termed a veritable 'Black Hole'. What they slept on I cannot say for certain, probably on heaps of straw with horse-cloths, and possibly soot sacks for 'happings'. Their sooty clothes they never doffed from beginning to end. These operations connected with the soot continued for a fortnight.

But when at length the work was completed the question came as to how the lads were to be restored to a state of cleanliness. They were as black as Hottentots. It was quite impossible for them to clean themselves, and so some one else must do it for them. And now the fun of the thing began. A huge scalding-tub was brought into requisition, into which the men plunged one after another like sheep into a 'wash-dyke'. The servant lasses then came with brushes and other cleansing articles and proceeded to operate on the lads and men with all the force at their command. The scene can be better imagined than described, and I must leave the reader to picture the process here employed for the eradication of soot from the human frame according to his own thinking.

Revd M.C.F. Morris

LIVING BY THE FRUIT OF THE SEA

Scarborough . . . derived its scaly, glittering harvest from the waves that could be seen rolling their long lines in exemplary formation. By the fruit of the sea it lived all the autumn, vying proudly with Aberdeen. The quays would be lined nearly every morning with ships, their brown sails furled, and often fleets would be seen under full sail, approaching. Nets bursting with fish, and empty barrels stood upon the stone platform, and the air was strong with the smell of salt and rope and fish, and tar and wood-smoke. The fishwives roared to each other across their tables, slimy and running in the morning sunlight, and the paving itself was slippery from the catch, soon to be smoked and dried. It was such a sight as this, perhaps, the memory of which inspired Thomas Nashe to write, in his *Lenten Stuffe*, 'In Prayse of the Red Herring.'

Osbert Sitwell

COLLECTING BIRDS' EGGS ON FLAMBOROUGH CLIFFS

If I sit down on the cliff top, where the chalk rises from below in high, tapering columns, I am not more than twenty yards from the ledges where the gulls sit crowded side by side; I can watch them lighting and taking wing, or waddling to and fro and stretching their long black necks towards each other. A little way beyond me a small wooden hut stands on

Birds' egg collectors, Flamborough cliffs

the grass near the edge of the cliff, and while I am wondering idly with what object it was placed there, I see that four men have emerged from it, and are sauntering along towards me. One carries a coil of rope which he pitches down upon the grass just above the precipice which I have been watching; while one of his companions drives into the ground two

Climbers on Bempton cliffs

pulley spikes, each carrying a wheel over which the rope will run with no risk of chafing, placing one spike dexterously at the extreme edge of the cliff. Meantime another man has been slipping over his legs and fastening tightly round his body a kind of sling sufficient to support his weight with comfort, and when his equipment is complete all the others sit down on the grass, holding firmly to the rope, while the climber lets himself go confidently over the cliff edge, and swings down easily among the birds. Far down the cool shadow of the white rock he drops towards the blue sea below, pausing every now and then as his quick eye catches the blue gleaming of an egg, which he transfers deftly to a canvas wallet by his side. And now he has dropped as far as he desires, and the most difficult part of his journey begins, for in going down he swung almost free of the cliff face, descending easily as the men above paid out the rope. But coming up strains every muscle in his agile, well-knit frame, and as he strikes out with his legs, catching now one and now another shelf of rock, on each of which his weight hangs for the fraction of an instant, the tension of his muscles is evident enough, and one realises in watching him how great must be the strength and the agility needed to accomplish the ascent. Seven eggs rewarded the bold climber, and as I moved away another man was about to try his luck.

Arthur H. Norway

Prince's Dock, Hull

A TOUR OF THE HULL DOCKS

Let us take a walk round some of the Hull docks, and try to realise what the import and export trade really means.

Here, in the Alexandra Dock, is a huge iron steamship into which coal is being shipped by means of electric coal hoists or by transporter belts. Its cargo of 5,000 tons is being taken on board at the rate of ten tons a minute. From the hold of another equally large ship grain is pouring into lighters ranged alongside. It will require five working days of ten hours each to discharge its cargo of 6,000 tons. Then the ship will take its place under the coal hoists, and its empty hold will be filled with an outgoing cargo of 'black diamonds.'

The Victoria Dock is mainly given up to vessels unloading timber from the White Sea and the Baltic, a large proportion of it being 'pit props' for the coal mines of Yorkshire and Lancashire.

In the Albert and William Wright Dock, as well as in the Alexandra Dock, are vessels discharging hundreds of cases of bacon and hams from the United States, or of frozen carcasses of sheep from South America. From the hold of another vessel are being brought up crate after crate of eggs from North Russia, from another bale after bale of wool from Australia. Lined up alongside another big steamship are dozens of agricultural engines and machines made by workmen in Gainsborough and Lincoln. In a few weeks' time they will be at work in the corn-fields of Russia.

Every day of the week we shall find ships giving up their cargoes of linseed and cottonseed from India, Egypt, or South Russia. But if we want to see the 'butter boats' emptied, we must be on the spot in the very early hours of a Monday morning. For these boats arrive from Denmark during the Sunday, and the week of transporting their cargoes to the lines of railway waggons that await their arrival begins with the last stroke of midnight. By four or five o'clock on the Monday morning the butter is on its way to all parts of the north of England. The cargo of one ship alone is sometimes consigned to as many as 300 separate stations.

Come for a walk along the Humber Dock or on the Riverside Quay and, according to the season of the year, we shall see unshipped cargoes of plums from Germany; new potatoes and other vegetables from Jersey, France, and Holland; cranberries from Russia; bananas from the Canary Isles; apples from Australia, Canada, and the United States; oranges, lemons, grapes, nuts, tomatoes and onions from Spain, Portugal and Italy.

Last of all we will pay a visit to the St Andrew's Dock, and watch the entrance and unloading of the steam trawlers and steam carriers of the Hull fishing fleets. From the fishing-grounds of the North Sea, the White Sea, and the stormy seas around Iceland each brings its 'catch.' As quickly as it can be brought up from the hold – tubs of plaice, turbot, halibut, codfish, ling, hake or herring – it is sold at auction to the fish buyers who attend from all the large towns of the north of England; and as quickly it is packed on board the waiting 'Fish Trains,' which will distribute it among the fifteen million people who live within reach of the port of Hull.

Horace B. Browne

Barges on the River Hull

KEEL-HAULING ON THE CANALS

We usually sailed along the canal to Crowle, Medgehall and Thorne, but when sailing was impossible we had a man and a horse to pull the keel from the hauling banks. We hired the horse marine, as we called him, from the canal towns by sending word with a passing keel. In Thorne we hired Martin Henry, who had only one horse, and led it himself. In Mexborough we hired from a family called Bisby, who owned fifteen or twenty horses, and charged roughly 1s a mile.

Sometimes the same horse marine would take us right through to Sheffield. When we reached Mexborough he would stable his horse at the lock-keeper's cottage and sleep himself on the lockers in our cabin. There were times when I had to sleep like that myself. We used to say that Dad could sleep on a clothes-line. He could have done too, and woken up at the right time, for he could wake at whatever time he wanted without an alarm clock. I never could!

Part of the horse marine's fee was his breakfast or dinner aboard the keel. Mother cooked when she was aboard, but if she was not, it was my job. These men had such huge appetites that Dad used to say that they only ate when they were hauling our keels.

When the horse marine was hauling he often walked backwards at the canal side of the horse, to keep an eye on the keel and to make sure that the line did not foul anything,

for if it had done, the horse would have fallen into the canal. The horse wore a strong but simple harness. It had a collar with a side trace at each side. These reached a little behind the horse, and were fastened to a piece of wood called a cobble-stick, and made especially for keel-hauling. In the middle was a hook which swivelled either way, and to which the horse line was fastened.

The rest of the harness consisted of a back band, which went from the collar along the back of the horse and ended with a loop for the horse's tail. Two other back bands led downwards from this one and supported the traces. The horse had a bridle with short reins, and a halter so that we could tie him up and prevent him from wandering off or falling into the canal whilst we were waiting our turn at the locks. We fastened the horse line, a short cotton line, to the mast or to a short pole called a neddy, which fitted into the lutchet if the mast had been taken down.

The horses knew exactly what to do with a loaded keel. They went slowly into the line until it was tight and then just lay against the line as if they were lying down.

It took a horse eight hours or more to pull a keel 10 miles, so there was no stopping to eat. It ate as it worked, out of a nose tin fastened by a rope which went over its head and which could be adjusted to any height. We put corn and chaff into the tin and damped it down so that the horse could not blow the chaff away. The feed was carried on the horse's own back, in a long, narrow corn bag made of sailcloth.

Often, after the poor creature had hauled for ten or eleven miles, it had to walk back with the horse marine riding so as to be ready for the next day's work, which meant a day of more than twelve hours for both horse and man.

The only change or rest it got was when hauling banks changed sides. At Kilnhurst on the river Don we had to hang on to the hauling banks while the horse was ferried across, but usually there was a bridge.

The horses had a poor time of it, and had a shorter life than most, for keel-hauling was a killing job. They were worked until their strength failed, then were sold to horse-dealers and put down, to end up as dog-food, fats and bone meal. I never heard of any being put out to grass or given honourable retirement.

Harry Fletcher

Market Place, Hull

'T'HORSE AT WRONG END'

A big brown mare once trod on my foot when I was leading. I gave a great yell, but had to limp on to the next bridge before I could get a rest. The average speed of that horse was 1¼ miles an hour, but it seemed like two hours before it lifted its foot. Two of my toes were black when I took my boot off, and I really thought they would fall off.

Another time the horse missed its footing and rolled down the bank into the water. I was much too weak to stop it, and

the banks were so steep that we could not get it out again, so we tied it to the back of the keel and towed it along. The journey was not without incident, and Dad had to stand some racket when we passed other boats.

'Hey up, Young Jim!' shouted one captain (since my dad was always known in this way even when he was in his sixties). 'Doesn't tha know tha's got t'horse at wrong end?'

The horse enjoyed it. There he was, having a cool swim while Dad pushed the keel with a boat-hook, the horse marine pulled from the hauling banks and I steered. The

Stonemason's yard, Ampleforth

SHOT HOLES

RUSSIAN OUTRAGE ON HULL TRAWLERS. SCENE AT ST ANDREWS DOCK HULL. S.R&C°

'Russian Outrage on Hull Trawlers', December 1904

accident happened near Sandall but we reached Doncaster, about three miles away, before we found a flat spot to haul the horse out, and even then it took six men to do the job.

If times were bad and we couldn't even afford a horse marine, or we were having to take an empty keel back to Hull, then we pulled the keel by hand, using a harness called a seal, made of a piece of sailcloth or leather about 3 in wide, with ropes attached to each end. These were tied to a thin cotton line called a manline, which was much lighter than a horse line. We put the seal across our chests and round our shoulders and leaned forward, getting as much weight as we could into the seal, and unlike the horse marine, we faced the way we were going. Mother and I pulled when the keel was empty, and could move it at a walking pace.

Sometimes we even used a boat-hook to get us along. We put the end with the hook on anything handy – another keel, a wall, the bottom of the canal – and then we pushed. We had two or three boat-hooks of different lengths, with a hook and a prong at one end and a pummel at the other. The pummel was about 3 in in diameter, and we put it against our shoulders and pushed or pulled by gripping the boat-hook with both hands.

Our progress along the canals, whether by sail, horse or hand, was always slowed up by the locks. The keel was lifted up twenty-eight locks between Hull and Sheffield, and old keelmen used to say that by the time a keel reached Sheffield it was as high as Holy Trinity Church in Hull.

Harry Fletcher

RATS AS BIG AS LARGE CATS

We spent a lot of our time catapulting at rats under the landing-stages. They were the biggest I have ever seen, as big as large cats, and at night when we were in bed we could hear them running about the decks. We had to take care they didn't get into the keel. Occasionally they did and we had to put down poison for them. I remember once seeing Mother going to the cupboard for a toy for my baby brother and putting her hand on a dead rat instead. She was up that ladder and out of the cabin hatch quicker than I could ever have been.

Harry Fletcher

Further evidence of the attack

OUTRAGE BY THE RUSSIAN NAVY

I was watching when the trawlers that had been fired on by the Russian Navy came in from sea. These trawlers were 'boxmen', or 'fleeters', because they sailed in a fleet and packed their catch into boxes, transferring it at about four o'clock in the morning to a carrier ship which took it straight to London. They always fished at night by the light of acetylene lamps, and the Russians had seen the ships and the flashing lights and thought the Japanese fleet was attacking them. They opened fire and had killed two fishermen before they realized their mistake. In the Boulevard at Hull there is a monument to these two men, and to a third who died of shock later.

Harry Fletcher

Chapter 7

PASTORS, PHYSICIANS AND SOLICITORS

'It is said that the parson knows a man at his best, the lawyer knows him at his worst, but that only the doctor knows him as he really is. This is true.' So claimed Dr R.W.S. Bishop who for some thirty years around the turn of the century served as a GP in the scattered communities of the north-western part of the county. In My Moorland Patients *he recorded his patients' foibles and idiosyncrasies with sympathy and wit, his professional poise disturbed only once when a 'Paul Pry' confided that he had spied on a case of incest. The good doctor 'hurried away in disgust'.*

The rudimentary health care available then is highlighted by Brenda English's recollection of her father carrying out surgery in his patients' homes in front of the kitchen fire. (After one such operation, the patient arrived at the doctor's house a few days later leading a cow, a gift in gratitude for the successful outcome of the kitchen surgery.)

Few lawyers of the time committed their memories to paper. A fortunate exception was C.J.F. Atkinson, a West Riding solicitor with a wry understanding of his clients, many of them well-to-do farmers who nevertheless, when required to sign or witness a legal document, would inscribe a wavering X. Within the profession, they were known as 'marksmen', from 'making their mark'. While discreetly protecting his clients' anonymity, Atkinson uncovers some interesting skeletons tucked away in their cupboards.

Other memoirs from the time testify to the central rôle of church and chapel in their parishioners' social life, particularly in the villages. Summer Garden Parties and Sunday School outings, Harvest Festival, carol singing at Christmas – regular rituals fostering a strong sense of community. And the pervading gloom we associate with Victorian religion was not entirely universal, as is proved by Christabel Burniston's recollections of her Wesleyan Sunday School in the East Riding.

Reluctantly, I have included only one extract in this book from Canon J.C. Atkinson's classic work Forty Years in a Moorland Parish, *partly because many extracts from it were included in my earlier volume in this series* The North Riding of 100 Years Ago, *and partly because a recent reprint has made his book widely available. Anyone who has not yet come across this mesmerizing account of the Canon's forty years as Rector of Danby in the North York Moors has a great treat awaiting them.*

Lane End Almshouses, Chapeltown, Leeds, c. 1910

KNOWING A MAN AS HE REALLY IS

It is said that the parson knows a man at his best, the lawyer knows him at his worst, but that only the doctor knows him as he really is. This is true. When man is sick and racked with bodily or mental pain, he recognises his frailty; all his artificiality and veneer depart for the while, and his true character is revealed. The country doctor who knows how to make use of this opportunity and tries to live up to the highest ideals of his profession, is a privileged being, wielding great power and bearing a great responsibility in his little kingdom. He sees Jack and Jill, whom he brought into the world, grow up and develop. He becomes the confidential friend of the family, the trusted adviser in important events, and the depositary of sacred secrets. His life is so rich in human problems that he can never be dull.

Reeth Board of Guardians in front of the workhouse

My neighbours perhaps differed more from one another in character, personality, and habits than human beings ordinarily do. Such differences were conspicuous in a sparsely populated country, and become exaggerated by isolation.

Dwellers in towns, like stones in the pot-hole of a river-bed, have all their edges and peculiarities rounded off.

In the country, on the other hand, there is so much elbow-room for everybody that individual eccentricities are accentuated, and the edges of character become sharp and rugged. Moreover, in the country, everybody knows everything about everybody and seeks to know more. Curiosity is rampant. It is said that country people will even look down the chimney to see what their neighbours are having for breakfast. An unused chimney sending forth for the nonce its volume of smoke advertises to the country-side that something unusual is on foot. 'Another chimbley smoking at Trotter's this morn.' 'What's up? Onnyways t'bairn isn't looked for yet awhile. Must be his sister fra Lunnon, or yon painting chap is there ageean.' Country curiosity is insatiable. Paul Prys abound. Eavesdropping is no disgrace. One salutes the passer-by in the dark, purely in order to recognise the voice and guess what his business may be. The village postman in those days would read all the correspondence he could, and then retail it for his neighbours' benefit. One local postman I knew made a sad blunder. After steaming two letters open he put the letters into the wrong envelopes, and of course there was trouble, which sent him back to cobbling and bitter reflections.

I knew of an incident where, to satisfy an extreme curiosity, a ladder was noiselessly ascended to the window of a particular bedroom. A statement was made to me once in confidence, so extraordinary and unbelievable, that I refused to credit it. I said, 'I don't believe a word of it. It's all rubbish.' 'It may be rubbish,' was the reply, 'but Ah see'd it all wi' me 'ain ees.' Then I realised what it meant to have seen with his own eyes, and hurried away in disgust. It was a case of incest.

R.W.S. Bishop

THE DOCTOR AS DICTATOR

With country doctors it is different. They are privileged to speak their mind, and to address patients in language which would give umbrage and offence from anyone else. I have heard village medicos pull up by the roadside on seeing a patient at work when he should be indoors, and reprove him thus: 'You great daft devil, what the —— are you doing outside? D—— it, I ordered you to stay in bed until I told you to get up. Get yourself indoors, or I'll take a stick to you!' And to others, who are hypochondriacs – 'What you want is not a bottle of what you call my "stuff", but to eat and drink less, and get out and do a good day's work. You'd be a lot worse if there was anything the matter with you.' This relationship between the old type of rural doctor and his patient is remarkable. He is accepted as a forthright dictator, who has no

Children's ward at Sheffield General Hospital, Christmas 1911

time for a humbug; who knows the skeleton in most family cupboards; and who is the kindest and most sympathetic of men when heart's-warmth and tenderness is called for.

J. Fairfax-Blakeborough

FIGHTING THE VACCINATION LAWS

In the middle of the eighties, I took part in the movement against compulsory vaccination. It may have been right or it may have been wrong, but we thought it wrong, and I joined up with a score or two more who went into the highways

and by-ways, talking like learned men on facts and figures, statistics and returns, without any fear despite sneers and jeers and uninformed opposition. Looking back on some newspaper cuttings of that time, I find the following, anent a public meeting in Huddersfield Market Place:–

Mr Turner strongly censured the Huddersfield Bench for their utter indifference to conscientious objectors, and urged it was cruel and vindictive to fine anti-vaccinators the full penalty whilst letting drunkards, wife-beaters, and others, guilty of real and inexcusable crimes against society, off with mitigated penalties. The rich magistrates required to read and study this question as well as the poor anti-vaccinators. Mr Cotton then recited 'Doctor, spare that child,' and Mr Turner his poem, 'For Conscience Sake,' in very good style, and were heartily applauded. A long discussion ensued, and the meeting which lasted two hours, was very successful.

So ran the report in the *Huddersfield Examiner*.

When my children started to come I followed up my belief by refusing to have them vaccinated. As a result, I was summoned on four different occasions. In those days the law was that you had to be summoned to shew cause why you didn't have your child vaccinated. Then it was followed by another for disobeying the order of the magistrates to have it vaccinated. The first cost 7/6, and the second cost what the magistrates thought proper up to 20/- and costs. There was also power under the Act for a layman – not a solicitor – to

Benson's butcher's shop, Potter Hill, Pickering

appear and defend another person, and I have appeared both for myself and for other folks. Of course, it was always without success. I remember going in my smock and clogs straight from the mill one forenoon to the Huddersfield Police Court to defend a fellow victim of the law. They gave me short shrift. I was expounding my opinion about the evils of vaccination when the Magistrates' Clerk cut me short. I challenged him that I had a right to speak thus in defending another man. He knew I knew that part of the law, and whilst I was continuing my speech and giving facts and figures, the magistrates said they wanted to hear no more, and inflicted the usual 20/- and costs. I was in my element, and scornfully said to the bench, 'It says Justitia at the head of your chairs, but there is no justice here.' A policeman got hold of my arm and pulled me away from the court seats. I protested, but he had me under physical control, and I continued to protest until he got me into the street.

I happened to be sold up because I wouldn't pay the 7/6 court costs, on an order being made. The police were very good to me. They kept sending an old neighbourly policeman up to get me to pay, or to get my wife to pay, but we didn't, and after many months they sent the police trap up and took our sewing machine, my present arm-chair, my wife's chair, a square table and three bedroom chairs, to be sold. They had a big trap load. The goods were taken to an auctioneer's saleroom and not sold outside our house as expected. This was to prevent any possible demonstration, for it had been arranged that when I was sold up, there should be a protest meeting. They 'old-manned' or out planned us, for in taking the goods to the saleroom they countered us, and prevented a protest meeting. Perhaps it was as well. When the goods were put up for sale the first bid was 1d. A broker then bid 5/-, and one of my colleagues, by arrangement, then bid £1, and as this covered the court costs and auctioneer's costs, the sale was over. The police were extra kind. They took all my goods and chattels back home, and the old village policeman seemed as pleased as Punch that all was over, and no trouble occurred. My old arm-chair and my wife's rocking chair still bear the mark of the Queen's bailiff who marked our goods before taking them to the sale.

Ben Turner

HEALTH OF THE WORKING CLASSES

Striking evidence of the low standard of physical efficiency which obtains among the working classes generally is afforded by the statistics which show the proportion of recruits applying for enlistment in the army who are rejected on account of physical unfitness. The writer has obtained detailed particulars regarding the medical examination of 3600 recruits who applied for enlistment at York, Leeds, and Sheffield, between 1897 and 1901. The proportion accepted and rejected was as follows:–

Recruiting Stations	Period	Number applying for Enlistment	Accepted	Rejected	Percentage rejected
York, Leeds and Sheffield	1897–1901	3600	2650	950	26½

Of those who were accepted 760, or 21 per cent, were first taken as 'specials.' 'Specials' are men who, although not up to standard when they apply for enlistment, are taken on trial, with a view to seeing whether a few months of army life, with its good and sufficient food, drill, and regular habits, will bring them up to standard. An officer of long experience in the army informed the writer that the improvement which a few months of army life makes in the physical condition of the majority of these 'specials' is most marked.

In order to arrive at the proportion of recruits whose physical condition was not up to the army standard when they applied for enlistment, the number of 'specials' must be added to the number rejected. If this be done it is found that out of 3600 recruits no less than 1710, or 47½ per cent, must be so classed. When it is borne in mind that, in order to obtain the required number of men, the army standards of health and physical development have been repeatedly lowered, and are now by no means high, the low standard of health amongst the working classes which the figures indicate becomes increasingly apparent.

The following are the present standards in some of the main arms of the service:–

	Minimum Height	Minimum Chest Measurement
Cavalry –	ft. in.	in.
Dragoons of the Line & Lancers	5 7	34
Hussars of the Line . . .	5 6	34
Infantry –		
Infantry of the line . . .	5 3	33
Minimum weight for all branches 115 lbs. (8 st. 3 lbs).		

The causes which led to the rejection of the 950 recruits were as follows:–

	Number	Per cent
Defective vision . . .	149	15.7
Defective hearing . . .	2	.2
Under-developed (*i.e.* chest, weight, or height).	297	31.1
Dull intellect . . .	3	.3
Many decayed teeth . . .	99	10.5
Deformed limbs . . .	110	11.6
Diseases . . .	290	30.6
	950	100.0

Although the proportion of recruits rejected on account of physical unfitness at the York, Leeds, and Sheffield recruiting stations (viz. 26½ per cent) may appear high, it is nevertheless below the average for the United Kingdom.

The following table, taken from the Annual Report of the Inspector-General of Recruiting for 1900 (p. 14), gives particulars, covering the whole of the United Kingdom, of the number of ordinary recruits who presented themselves for medical examination during the past five years, the number of those who were rejected, and the percentage of rejections:–

	1896	1897	1898	1899	1900
Numbers medically inspected . . .	54,574	59,986	66,501	68,059	88,402
Numbers rejected					
For various ailments	11,251	12,630	13,969	13,501	13,788
For want of physical development . . .	11,781	10,183	9,318	8,892	9,317
Total rejected	23,032	22,813	23,287	22,393	23,105
Percentage of rejections					
For various ailments	20.6	21.0	21.0	19.8	16.9
For want of physical development . . .	21.6	17.0	14.0	13.1	11.1
Total	42.2	38.0	35.0	32.9	28.0

It will be noted that so far from the percentage of rejections in 1900 being unusually high, it is considerably below the average. The following explanation of this circumstance is given in the Report above named:– 'All officers concerned in recruiting have instructions not to send a recruit up for medical examination unless there is a reasonable probability of his passing. The very great reduction in the percentage of rejections – from 42 in 1896 to 28 in 1900 – shows that these orders have been carried out with marked success. The reduction is also due partly to the reduction of standard of which mention has already been made, and partly to the fact that owing to the war more matured recruits came forward for enlistment.'

B. Seebohm Rowntree

SANITARY ARRANGEMENTS AT WORK

Over the whole city the common privy and ashpit is the rule, water closets the exception; in no part has a water closet system been adopted. Many of the larger houses have water closets inside and privies outside. During the past ten years the condition of the privies and ashpits has been considerably improved. In many of the worst places they have been removed and replaced by water closets; in other places ashpits have been abolished, refuse being placed in any moveable receptacle and put into the scavengers' carts whenever they are in the neighbourhood. Most, if not all, the smaller houses in the city have the drain inlet

Knaresborough Castle

Micklegate Bar, York

disconnected from the sewer, the sink pipe, generally the only inlet, being made to discharge on to a trapped gulley outside. To a very considerable extent the back yards have been laid with some impervious material, flags, cement, or asphalte, and generally the surface drainage has been much improved.

There is no systematic collection of night soil or other refuse; all is left to individual action. By diligent inspection accumulations are kept down; nevertheless the rule is to retain the contents of privies and ashpits for weeks and months. In many places the contents of these receptacles have to be carried through the houses and deposited in the street previous to removal. New streets have been formed with back roads. Although in by far the greater number of instances each house has its own separate privy or water closet, yet in numerous cases these conveniences are used by the members of two or more families, and still more frequently, whilst the privy is separate, the ashpit and privy vault is common to two or more.

All new privies are required to have the floor of the vault laid with concrete and the walls built in cement. Such is the general character of the sanitary arrangements of houses throughout the city.

'Report on the Prevalence of Typhoid Fever in York during the Year 1886'

Nurse Hetty Mason, Doncaster

ROMAN BATHS.
The famous Plunge Bath.

The water is mellifluent, diaphanous, luminous, transparent, pellucid, immaculate, and unequalled in purity. It is vitalising, animating exhilarating, resuscitating, enthusing sustaining refreshing, invigorating, delightful and delicious as a bath It is instinct with life, and is seven degrees colder than ordinary well water. It strengthens the muscles and tissues, and improves the general condition, nutrition, and tone of the body, and gives increased energy, and capacity for work.

The famous Plunge Bath, Ben Rhydding Spa

EVENING ENTERTAINMENT AT THE SPA

We found the inmates of Ben Rhydding assembled in the dining-hall having tea, with meat or eggs. After this was over we all went to the drawing-room, when presently a very clever reading from *Martin Chuzzlewit* was given by one of the visitors. Then there was some good singing; later on some of the young people danced; at ten the lights began to be put out in the drawing-room, and people went to their rooms or else to the dining-room again, where was spread another plentiful meal of bread and butter, bread and milk, and gruel; or wine and beer could be had if required. The simple diet and regular hours, for lights are expected to be out by eleven o'clock, doubtless benefit delicate people; but the pure air, and the refreshment effected by such a constant sight of this beautiful hill-girt valley, are themselves lifegiving. A few weeks spent at Ben Rhydding seem to effect a complete change in the system. I have seen delicate women, scarcely able to walk feebly round the garden on their first arrival, become strong enough to walk to the Hunting-tower, a lovely point in the heart of the moor at some distance from the house; beyond this tower are the mounds of a British village. But for the first week the air is almost too

exhilarating, and exhausts as much as it revives; it is the after and permanent effect that makes a visit to Ben Rhydding so thoroughly beneficial.

Thomas and Katherine McQuaid

SURGERY IN FRONT OF THE KITCHEN FIRE

As only three surgical beds were available at the Whitby Cottage Hospital, my Father usually carried out operations at the houses of his patients, and on these occasions my Mother generally accompanied him. The folding operating table was then set up in front of the kitchen fire, the instruments placed in lysol, and cotton wool swabs in a bowl of boiled water. Thomas would administer chloroform, then rush round the table and operate at top speed, till the patient began to show signs of coming round, when he would either prolong the anaesthetic or stitch up the wound, according to the stage reached. Almost all emergencies and major operations were carried out in this way, strangely enough usually with satisfactory results, though medical readers will note the absence of aseptic precautions. Yet one must remember that Thomas and Louie had only just emerged from the London Hospital, where carbolic sprays and sponges had been the order of the day, while gloves were not yet tolerated by many surgeons since these, being much too thick when first introduced, impeded their dexterity.

Brenda H. English

FOLLY OF THE GREAT POWERS AT WHITEHALL

One great obstacle to useful progress in local government is the prejudice of the people against changes in domestic matters, even when it affects their own health. I remember a row of cottages, where the only water supply was from a trough by the road side and almost level with the ground. Horses drank at it, and cows put their feet into it, but still the cottagers were content to fetch this water into their houses with buckets. The owner offered to lay pipes to the spring, which fed the trough, and to bring the water to kitchen taps. The cottagers all objected to this as a 'new fangled notion.' They said, 'We can see what we are getting from that there trough, but we shan't see inside a tap!' When the owner's wife pointed out that the water in the trough was sometimes brown and brackish, one of the lusty housewives replied, 'All the better, it tak's less tea to give it a taste.'

On the other side, it must be said that progressive thought is often discouraged by the cast-iron ideas which prevail in some of the Government offices, which supervise local authorities. These Great Powers at Whitehall do not realize that all localities are not alike, and that a reasonable liberty to adapt policy to local needs would be helpful. For instance, it is a rule that every school must have a playground. Now

The water carrier delivers to the village of Sinnington

Children's home on the moors, Summerbridge

Pupils at St James's School, Thornton, Bradford, 1898

Election postcard issued by George Fentress, candidate in Pickering
Council Election, 1910

there was a pretty little village school, high up the dales, with an acre of open green on one side and a thousand acres of moorland on the other. No school in England had more room for play. The managers took great pride in it, the children were healthy, bright and well taught. It seemed to be all that a little rural school could be. But one day there came an inspector's report which took the heart out of managers, teachers and everyone. The school would be condemned unless it was provided with playgrounds – two of them, one little yard for the boys and another little yard for the girls. The managers protested that the children all played on the moor and the green. No matter. 'The Board' could not understand – town schools needed fenced playgrounds, so all schools needed them. And so the managers had to enclose two little patches of land outside the school with stone walls. These cost money which was needed for other things, and of course they were never used. The boys and girls play all together on the moor and chase one another through the heather yet. But Whitehall was satisfied, and those little walls are monuments of its rule to this day.

I could write pages on the slogan of 'economy' in local government. Many people have the fixed idea that any dodge to save money for to-day is economy – no matter what happens next. A Fire Brigade committee in a small town once had to appoint a new fireman, in the place of one who had resigned. They set about their job, on 'economy' lines, by sizing up the uniform which the retiring man had sent back, then measured the new applicants, and appointed a man whom the clothes would fit, without any regard to his fitness to wear them. They saved a tailor's bill for uniform, but the new man spoiled five times that value of apparatus, at the next fire, by sheer incompetence.

C.J.F. Atkinson

ONE OF THE STRONGEST OF OUR BISHOPS

No better training for the position of a Diocesan Bishop can be had than that of Domestic Chaplain to a Bishop or Archbishop. Such a training had Dr Eden, the present Bishop of Wakefield. Ordained in 1878, he became in the following year Domestic Chaplain to Dr Lightfoot, Bishop of Durham. For eleven years he was intimately associated with this great Bishop, first for four years as Resident Chaplain in the Bishop's Palace and afterwards for seven years as Vicar of Bishop Auckland. Here it was that Dr Eden learned that knowledge of the Church's needs and possibilities, that self-restraint coupled with living zeal, that invaluable power of knowing and dealing with men, that makes him, while the youngest, one of the strongest of our Bishops.

In 1890, the late Archbishop Benson appointed him Canon and Archdeacon of Canterbury and Suffragan Bishop of Dover. Thus at the age of thirty-seven he was in a position of great responsibility. He soon, however, made his influence felt throughout the Diocese of Canterbury. Hither and thither he went; and town and country village saw the Bishop warmly supporting, and often inaugurating, good works; confirming, teaching, preaching; ever ready with advice and help; and wherever he went infusing life into the Church's work.

To leave the beautiful Cathedral Close of Canterbury and the fair fields of Kent in order to live in Wakefield and to work amidst the smoke of the manufactories of the West Riding must have been hard for Dr and Mrs Eden. Yet the Bishop went to his Northern Diocese with all the enthusiasm of one who had been born in the North of England, and who knew, and loved the men of the North.

Not only is Bishop Eden an excellent man of business, a good organizer, and a clear thinker, but he is also a man of deep personal piety. His sermons and addresses, as well as his general conversation, show the earnestness of his life. His influence for good is felt by all who come in contact with him.

As the son-in-law of Canon Ellison it is natural that Doctor Eden should take a deep interest in the temperance question. Under him the Church of England Temperance Society is being thoroughly organized in the Wakefield Diocese.

Yorkshire Men of Mark, 1898

BISHOP OF WAKEFIELD, GEORGE RODNEY EDEN, D.D.

The Bishop of Wakefield, George Rodney Eden, DD

THE EXCESSIVE POWER OF PRAYER

One Sunday in spring, after a month of devastating drought which was stunting the wheat and withering the grass, my grandfather led the farming worshippers in praying for rain. This they did in solos, unison and hymn-singing.

On the Monday it rained; gentle generous drops giving heart to the soil and greening the grass. On Tuesday, Wednesday and Thursday it rained without a break in the clouds. On Friday and Saturday the wind and rain lashed the corn on to the ground and floated the straw in the stackyard. On Sunday evening water dripped from clothes and boots on to the kitchen floor. It was the foreman's first chance to speak publicly to his God. Holding his arms high above his head he raged in his rolling dialect: 'O Lord last week we prayed for

Wesleyan garden party, Kirkbymoorside, July 1912

rain but this is ower doing it!' The rebuke evidently worked for they left the farm kitchen that Sunday evening in a benign red sunset.

The Carnaby station-master specialised in children's services but had little use for the 'Gentle Jesus, meek and mild' sops usually given to children. His faith burned with the fear of God and the Devil. Standing behind the lectern, his head nearly touching one of the cheese-cloth-covered hams, he chased the flies away as he threatened hell to the children who were squatting cross-legged on the red brick floor, looking angelic in their Sunday best.

'And tha'll go to 'ell as sure as I kill that fly!' he called out as he brought his fist down to demonstrate mortality. The fly flew off to the over-hanging ham and following its flight the preacher accepted defeat. 'Dang it. Ah's missed it; ther's chance for thee yet!'

On another occasion, when all the benches and chairs were filled with children for a Whitsuntide service, he tried out another hell-bent ploy: his forefinger wagging at three culprits: 'The divel is on a long chain, but he can reach *you* . . . and he can reach *YOU* . . . and he can reach *YOU!* To which the third boy, sitting as far away from the preacher as he could, called out: 'Bugger mu'd as well be *loose!*'

Testimony services were a significant feature of the country Wesleyan meetings. Anyone could stand and report on God's mysterious and marvellous ways. It was a chance for the women to have a say too and so on this summer evening, when it was easy for old Mrs Barmby to walk from her cottage to the farm, she was moved to heave herself from her seat and say in her slow trembling East Riding voice: 'As Ah sat on the privy seat this morning, Ah couldn't 'elp thinking 'ow fearfully and 'ow wunderfully we was made.'

Christabel Burniston

CAPTAIN OF THE BELFRY

In the churchyard, which slopes gently down towards the river, is a stone pillar, surmounted by a dial. Here, in olden days, stood the churchyard cross; from which 'Billy' Pickersgill, the parish clerk, nicknamed 'Dabbish-it,' from his habit of using that ejaculation, announced to the congregation, as they passed through the graveyard, the coming events of the week:– 'Oyez! oyez! oyez! This is ta

Methodists from Hungate Church, Pickering. On the left is Revd Alfred Vine who wrote the hymn 'O breath of God, breathe on me now'

The parish church, Sheffield

give all of ye notice that a vestry meeting will be held at Brigg end ta morn at neet, to appoint t' owerseers an t' surveyors, an' examin t' books.' A noted bellringer, Old Billy was also named 'Captain of the belfry.' In past days the Burnsall ringers were noted for their performances. One, who has now passed to the majority, said, 'I have often listened to their sweet music on clear, moonlight summer nights, when a gentle breeze wafted the silvery sounds up the dale, and myriad mountain echoes prolonged the melody.'

Some years after Billy Pickersgill's death, Peter Riley officiated as sexton and clerk, and was also famous on the double bass. Once during a service, when the only persons present were the preacher and sexton, the clergyman began,

'Dearly beloved brethren,' but Peter cried out, 'Nay, nay, ye moant say "brethren," ye mun say "dearly beloved Pete."' Of another remarkable character, Parson Alcock, many droll stories are related. On one occasion some mischievous person mixed the leaves of his sermon: after delivering two pages he came to a long pause; then, addressing the congregation, said, 'Someone has mixed my sermon, – however, I will read it as it is and you can digest it when you get home.'

The Revd Patrick Stewart was once placed in the same awkward position. On opening his manuscript he found the first page or two had been eaten away. 'My brethren,' he said, 'I find the mice have made free with the beginning of my sermon, so that I cannot tell you where the text is to be

Harvest festival, Marfleet

found; but we will just begin where the mice have left off, and find out the text as we go along.'

Edmund Bogg

A REALLY CHRISTIAN ACT

I was once called to the sick-bed of a well-to-do farmer to make his will. He had a grown-up family. Then, after his first wife's death, he had married a middle-aged housekeeper, a very intelligent woman, who had known better days but had taken a situation because she had no other means of livelihood. The farmer's will gave a modest, but comfortable, income for her during the rest of her life. Shortly afterwards the farmer died, and after the funeral I went to the house to read the will. The widow listened to it without a word. As the family were leaving she called me into another room and said, 'I shall not take that annuity. Before I came here, my husband had another housekeeper, a younger woman than I, and good-looking, too. He ought to have married her, but he did not, and she had to leave. Now she had a little boy to keep – his child. I did not know about this till he fell ill, and then he kept saying that he had not

always done what he ought. A letter came from the other woman pressing for more money as she was in want. I had to open it. He was too ill to do anything and could not answer. The night before he died was very stormy. Through the rain and the wind I heard a knock at the door, a woman's voice, and the cry of a child. I dared not open the door. I sat alone by his bedside thinking what I ought to do. I made up my mind then. I won't take the money. That young woman ought to have been in my place as his wife. She and the child ought to have been provided for, and they shall be, so far as I can do it. Here is her letter. Find her, please, and tell nobody, but tell her that I am making this money over to her. Yes, I will sign any document about it that you wish, but find her as soon as you can and let her know that she need not fear want. She ought to have been here in my place, and she must have the money. I can get another situation and keep myself, she cannot with his child in her arms.'

With a little kindly help from the police, I traced the other woman in a distant town. She had faced her trouble bravely, kept respectable and was just about to marry a decent workman to whom she had frankly told the whole of her story. They were greatly relieved and helped by the little annuity, which I paid regularly whilst the widow lived. I do not know how she maintained herself, but she never told her relatives what had been done with the money, for, when she died, a niece came to inquire about it. I told her what had been done, and produced the authority signed by the widow. The niece read it with tears in her eyes and then said, 'Well, it's just like my aunt. She was a real Christian.'

C.J.F. Atkinson

Laying the first tram rail, Porter Street, Hull, 1898

Fisher girl on the beach at Whitby

Chapter 8

TRAVELLING THE BROAD ACRES

'*T*raffic alters everything.' In the television films he made in the 1960s, John Betjeman repeated those words like a mantra as he mournfully chronicled the violation of once-peaceful village streets and the desecration of ancient market towns. A comparison of many of the places shown in this book with how they look today bears out the late Poet Laureate's indictment of the internal combustion engine (or rather our submission to its demands), as the single most destructive force of the twentieth century.

It is difficult now to fully comprehend how quiet the countryside was one hundred years ago. In 1899, Arthur H. Norway could walk along the Great North Road in south Yorkshire and reflect on 'its deserted ways which were once so full of noisy life'. Now 'only cyclists and ragged beggarmen' or 'yonder sleepy farmer jogging home from Doncaster in his gig' disturbed the peace of 'the broad old highway running straight and smooth between wide grassy borders'. Similarly, the old coaching road from Pickering to Whitby, according to J.E. Morris's North Riding of Yorkshire, was 'now seldom used' and he warned cyclists from travelling anywhere in the eastern moorlands where the roads were 'horribly loose and stony'.

If the number of travel books about Yorkshire is anything to go by, late Victorians were undeterred by such difficulties. Walking tours were very popular though few emulated R.N. and J.N. (later revealed as the brothers Robert and John Naylor) who walked from John o'Groats to Land's End in 1888, passing through York and Sheffield on the way. These years also saw the golden age of cycling with most towns of any size boasting a cycling club. Many travel books, like Arthur Norway's Highways and Byways in Yorkshire, were specifically directed at cyclists.

In the cities, trams were speedily replacing the old horse-drawn omnibuses but the most popular form of transport was the railway. The network was then at its most extensive, a cat's-cradle of lines that criss-crossed the county and penetrated deep into the major Dales. Only in Swaledale was the advance of the Iron Horse halted at Richmond in 1846 by the hostile terrain of the upper dale beyond. Cheap Day Excursions brought the workers of Leeds and Hull within easy reach of the east coast resorts – except for Saltburn-by-the-Sea where 'excursionists' were barred by the promoters of this tailor-made, middle-class resort developed in the 1860s.

The road from Askrigg

A CONTENTED ROAD MENDER

From Askrigg there is a road that climbs up from the end of the little street at a gradient that looks like 1 in 4, but it is really less formidable. Considering its steepness the surface is quite good, but that is due to the industry of a certain road-mender with whom I once had the privilege to talk when, hot and breathless, I paused to enjoy the great expanse that lay to the south. He was a fine Saxon type, with a sunburnt face and equally brown arms. Road-making had been his ideal when he was a mere boy, and since he had obtained his desire he told me that he couldn't be happier if he were the King of England. And his contentment seemed to me to be based largely upon his intense pleasure in bringing the roads to as great a perfection as his careful and thinking labour could compass. He did not approve of steamrollers, for his experience had taught him that if the stones were broken small enough they bound together quickly enough. Besides this, he disapproved of a great camber or curve on the road which induces the traffic to keep in the middle, leaving a mass of loose stones on either side. The result of his work may be seen on the highway from Askrigg to Bainbridge, where a conspicuous smoothness has come to a road that was recently one of the most indifferent in the district. Perhaps he may eventually be given the maintenance of the way over the Buttertubs Pass; and if he ever induces that road to become a little more civilized, this enthusiastic workman will gain the appreciation of the whole neighbourhood.

Gordon Home

ADVICE TO FEMALES PILGRIMATING WENSLEYDALE

I should advise all persons who pilgrimate the valley, if it is but for a day, to take with them an extra pair of shoes and stockings; for whether they visit fall or fell, they are pretty sure to get wetshod in seeking the best points of view. Besides, by wading a beck here and there, one avoids many a long and weary detour; and no harm follows being wetshod if you only change your foot-gear as soon as your march is done. The walking tourist will find it very convenient to have his light

Elijah Allen, 'licensed to let post-horses', with his family outside their shop in Gayle

marching-kit sent by the Mail-cart that goes up and down the valley every day, and calls at the principal villages on the route.

Females pilgrimating Wensleydale, on foot, will not 'merrily hent the stile-a' so long as the present preposterous form of petticoat prevails. A distinguished foreigner remarks: 'It is ridiculous to call woman's the softer sect when they are hooped with steel, and it is visible to the naked eye that are a deal more sterner than men's'. The stiles of Wensleydale are narrow slits in the walls, on the average from six to eight inches wide; and some I saw measured only four inches.

George Hardcastle

SONOROUS PRESENCE OF PACK-HORSES

Before the railway extensions, twenty years ago, Hawes was one of the most inaccessible places in the kingdom, being sixteen miles distant from the nearest station. The packhorse traffic lingered in this neighbourhood long after it had ceased in other parts of England. Handloom weaving was an old local industry, and when a sufficient number of pieces were ready, they were gathered up and conveyed by teams of pack-

Hawes, capital of Upper Wensleydale

A freak accident on the Beggar's Bridge, Glaisdale

horses over the mountains to Settle, and thence by the road to Bradford and other West Riding towns. Discharging their loads they would return laden with warp, weft, size and other articles. Occasionally they crossed by the old Cam pass – a wild rough road in misty or wet weather – but their presence was generally known by the tinkling of the bells, which could be heard at a good distance, and at the head of the pass far down Langstrothdale. When the traffic ceased, hundreds of these sonorous pack-bells were sold for old metal, and the brokers' for a time were full of them. Each bell weighed from 1lb to 2lb.

Harry Speight

GLAISDALE: THE BEGGAR'S BRIDGE

I come to a party of anglers trying their luck in a noted piece of water, called 'Dead Man's Pool,' and a few yards further on the celebrated Beggar's Bridge comes into view. There hangs a voluminous story regarding the history of this far-famed bridge, but the gist of it lies in the following lines:–

The rover came back from a far distant land,
And claimed from the maiden her long-promised hand,
But he built, ere he won her, the bridge of his vow,
And the lovers of Egton pass over it now.

What a delightful span it is, how light but yet how strong! and placed in lovely surroundings. To the wagoner we should say it is a terror, as, owing to its narrow width and abrupt rise, several accidents have taken place at this spot. We mention one in particular, in which the first horse of a tandem by some mischance fell over the bridge, and was suspended in mid-air till suffocated by its collar. Strange to say an enterprising local photographer was fortunate enough to obtain a picture of this extraordinary event.

Michael Heavisides

RIPON: A STARTLING CURFEW

I am startled by a long-drawn-out blast on a horn, and, looking out of my window, which commands the whole of

Market Place, Ripon, with the town hall to the right of the obelisk

The Royal Hotel, Harrogate

the market-place, I can see beneath the light of a lamp an old-fashioned figure wearing a three-cornered hat. When the last quavering note has come from the great circular horn, the man walks slowly across the wet cobblestones to the obelisk, where I watch him wind another blast just like the first, and then another, and then a third, immediately after which he walks briskly away and disappears down a turning. In the light of morning I discover that the horn was blown in front of the Town Hall, whose stucco front bears the inscription: 'Except ye Lord keep ye cittie, ye Wakeman waketh in vain.'

Gordon Home

HARROGATE: 'ALL SORTS AND CONDITIONS OF INVALIDS'

Soon after passing Starbeck we come to Harrogate's extensive common known as the Stray. We follow the grassy space, when it takes a sharp turn to the north, and are soon in the centre of the great watering-place. Among the buildings that rise up in imposing masses on each side of us we can see no traces of anything that is not of recent date, and we find nothing at all to suggest that the place really belongs to Yorkshire.

Walking or being pulled in bath-chairs along the carefully-made paths are all sorts and conditions of invalids, and interspersed among them are numbers of people who, if they have any ailments curable by the waters, are either in very advanced stages of convalescence or are extremely expert in hiding any traces of ill-health.

There is one spot in Harrogate that has a suggestion of the early days of the town. It is down in the corner where the valley gardens almost join the extremity of the Stray. There we find the Royal Pump Room that made its appearance in early Victorian times, and its circular counter is still crowded every morning by a throng of water-drinkers. We wander through the hilly streets and gaze at the pretentious hotels, the baths, the huge Kursaal, the hydropathic establishments, the smart shops, and the many churches, and then, having

seen enough of the buildings, we find a seat supported by green serpents, from which to watch the passers-by. A white-haired and withered man, having the stamp of a military life in his still erect bearing, paces slowly by; then come two elaborately dressed men of perhaps twenty-five. They wear brown suits and patent boots, and their bowler hats are pressed down on the backs of their heads. Then nursemaids with perambulators pass, followed by a lady in expensive garments, who talks volubly to her two pretty daughters. When we have tired of the pavements and the people, we bid farewell to them without much regret, being in a mood for simplicity and solitude, and go away towards Wharfedale with the pleasant tune that a band was playing still to remind us for a time of the scenes we have left behind.

Gordon Home

A PROBLEM WITH THE BOOTS

We continued along the valley of the River Ouse until we arrived at the city of York. We were very much impressed with the immense size and grandeur of the great Minster, with its three towers rising over two hundred feet in height. We were too late to see the whole of the interior of this splendid old building, but gazed with a feeling of wonder and awe on one of the largest stained-glass windows in the world, about seventy feet high, and probably also the oldest, as it dated back about five hundred years.

We could not explore the city further that afternoon, as the weather again became very bad, so we retreated to our inn, and as our sorely-tried shoes required soling and heeling, we arranged with the 'boots' of the inn to induce a shoemaker friend of his in the city to work at them during the night and return them thoroughly repaired to the hotel by six o'clock the following morning. During the interval we wrote our letters and read some history, but our room was soon invaded by customers of the inn, who were brought in one by one to see the strange characters who had walked all the way from John o' Groat's and were on their way to the Land's End, so much so that we began to wonder if it would end in our being exhibited in some show in the ancient market-place, which we had already seen and greatly admired, approached as it was then by so many narrow streets and avenues lined with overhanging houses of great antiquity. We were, however, very pleased with the interest shown both in ourselves and the object of our walk.

Wednesday, October 25th
The boots awoke us early in the morning, only to say that he had sent a messenger unsuccessfully into the town for our shoes; all the consolation he got was that as soon as they were finished, his friend the shoemaker would send them down to the hotel. It was quite an hour after the time specified when they arrived, but still early enough to admit of our walking before breakfast round the city walls, which we found did not encircle the town as completely as those of our county town of Chester. Where practicable we explored them, and saw many ancient buildings, including Clifford's Tower and the beautiful ruins of St Mary's Abbey. We also paid a second visit to the ancient market-place, with its quaint and picturesque surroundings, before returning to our inn, where we did ample justice to the good breakfast awaiting our arrival.

R.N. and J.N.

Bootham Bar, York

Hull Grocers' Walking Race

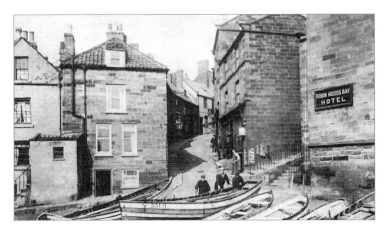

King Street, Robin Hood's Bay

ROBIN HOOD'S BAY: THE PATRIARCH OF THE PLACE

Everywhere huge nets were stretched out to dry. Rosy-cheeked children and pigs were plentiful, playing about promiscuously; sometimes a small bit of garden is walled up above the pathway, and is gay with sweet-william and snapdragon. We crossed the steep street to the opposite side of the town, and began to mount the broken, grassed cliff; on one side we found a steep flight of steps leading to the last cottage in the place. Its door stood open, a bit of fire on the hearth behind him showed a cobbler at his work in a low-roofed tiny room. He looked as if he might have been sitting there for years, a bit of dark wrinkled still-life, seemingly unconscious of passers-by.

Outside, in front of the brown-shuttered window, was a row of huge covered tubs, and beyond, a plot of brilliant orange marigolds sloping up to a potato ground which encroached on the moor. We climbed a little higher and got a grand view of the bay, with its stretch of silver sands and the bold cliffs rising from them. At our feet, and clinging up the side of the cliff, which seems to have been partially hollowed out to hold it, is the quaint little bay town.

Two old fishermen, one with long silver-white hair reaching to his shoulders, were sitting on the brow of the cliff when we reached it. They were quite ready to talk, and pointed out to us a yawl at the usual landing-place, just now inaccessible on account of a high tide. The yawl, they said, had brought coals to the town, but these could not be landed. Folk must wait, one of the men told us, till the carts and wheel-barrows of the place could reach the boat.

'There's nobbut little fishing now in t' bay,' he said.

'T' lads is at t' seea,' said the white-haired man; 'they'se at t' Baltic and such like;' and then he added with a grand air, 'Ah've seean t' Baltic.'

His companion, who looked ten years younger, and who was trying to keep in order a red-cheeked, strong-willed boy about four years old, said:

'He's seean t' Baltic an' ivvery place, an' he's aughty-foive;' then he looked as if he thought we ought to do homage to this patriarch of the place.

Thomas and Katherine McQuaid

The town crier, Whitby, 1904

WHITBY: THE OLD BELLMAN

The old bellman was amusing enough, one might have thought, as he announced day after day the time of the departure of the steamer for the next port. He was a lame man, having a lame foot supported by an iron construction, and he had a most extraordinary way of announcing his message. It ran somewhat like this: 'The steamer *Emu* (this was delivered in the treble) will leave the pier-side, Whitby (this was delivered in a comparatively natural voice) at eleven o'clock for Scarborough (this was in a lower key). Fare two and sixpence each.' (This was in the most astounding *basso profundo*.) But he was still more amusing when enlivened by liquor. On one occasion he was sent forth to announce an exchange of pulpits between the Presbyterian minister and the Congregational one. The actual announcement was fairly correct, I believe, but the final line of the announcement seems to have been muddled up in his mind, for it ran: 'Congregationalists will please roll up.'

William E. Anderton

'Morning and Evening', a classic study by Frank Meadow Sutcliffe, Whitby

WHITBY: 'A VERY PRIMITIVE PLACE'

I am really at Whitby, whither I have been every summer but '85 for the last six years. This will tell you how much I like it. A very primitive place it is, and the manners and ways of its people much like those of New England. . . . 'Tis a wonderfully picturesque place, with the bleaching bones of its Abbey standing aloof on the bluff, and dominating the country for leagues. Once, they say, the monks were lords as far as they could see. The skeleton of the Abbey still lords it over the landscape, which was certainly one of the richest possessions they had, for there never was finer. Sea and moor, hill and dale; sea dotted with purple sails and white (fancy mixes a little in the purple perhaps), moors flushed with heather in blossom, and fields yellow with corn, and the dark heaps of trees in every valley blabbing the secret of the stream that fain would hide to escape being the drudge of man. I know not why, wind has replaced water for grinding, and the huge water-wheels, green with moss and motionless, give one a

sense of repose after toil that, to a lazy man like me, is full of comfort. . . . I wish you could see the 'yards' – steep flights of stone steps hurrying down from the West cliff and the East, between which the river (whose name I never can remember) crawls into the sea, and where I meet little girls with trays bearing the family pies to the baker, and groups of rosy children making all manner of playthings of a bone or a rag. And I wish you could see the pier, with its throng of long-booted fishermen, looking the worthy descendants of the Northmen who first rowed their ships into the shelter of the cliffs, and named the place. And I wish you could breathe the ample air of the moors – I mean with me.

James Russell Lowell, letter to Miss Sidgwick, 18 August 1887

SALTBURN-BY-THE-SEA: 'FACILITIES FOR A QUIET RUSTICATION'

Little more than half-a-dozen years ago, Saltburn consisted of but a few insignificant cottages – the habitations of fishermen, and presented an appearance wild and desolate indeed; but the genius of modern art and taste has been at work, and transformed the wilderness into a smiling garden. It must be confessed that it was a bold idea to originate a watering-place of Saltburn; but, in this matter, the same sound judgment was displayed as has charactertised the policy of the promoters in all their vast undertakings. The word 'failure' has no place in their vocabulary; whatever they have yet undertaken has prospered, and why should not Saltburn?

In fixing upon Saltburn as the *locale* of a new marine resort, considerable discrimination was evinced as to the requirements of such a spot; and we venture to say, that there is scarcely any other watering place in Britain that can boast of so many of what we may call the *natural* requisites for a first-class sea-side resort. A large proportion of those who periodically frequent watering places are led thither, not so much for sea-bathing, as for a brief cessation from the toils and anxieties of business, and their choice naturally falls upon those spots which afford the most facilities for a quiet rustication. Such a place is Saltburn, as it blends the advantages of the sea-side with the rural enjoyments of the country.

Samuel Gordon

EXPEDITION TO A FLYING BENT GRASS BOG

I had a most interesting expedition yesterday. The weather was fine but blustery.

I started from here at 7.30 and trained to Goathland where I have not been since last September. There were only a few of us to walk to Levisham *via* Fen Bogs. I had a special permit to walk on the railway which, as you know, passes through

Saltburn-by-the-Sea, a tailor-made resort created in the 1860s

the fen. My observations of the fen have been confined to passing glimpses from the train, and to my surprise I found it was a vast Molinia or Flying Bent Grass Bog, interspersed with beds of Gale, Heather, Reeds, Rushes, Reed Mace, patches of Marsh Twayblade, Marsh Cinquefoil, and many plants unknown to me.

The bog was not very wet, strange to say, not where the Molinia was growing. The steep slopes of the dale were gashed by channels down which the recent torrential rains must have thundered. I kept sending you little wishes all the way, and herewith send you some Heather and Gale to sweeten our anniversary.

I found a blindworm asleep, and two vipers very wide awake. I pointed one out to a gentleman, a lay-reader, Sunday-school teacher, a tee-totaller, non-smoker, an instructor of the young, and to my amazement he most ferociously attacked the inoffensive reptile, battering it on the head and back with a stick until it was lifeless. What had been a graceful sinuous gliding organism of marvellous beauty, became in the hands of a believer in God's works a shapeless bruised mass. I felt disgusted, and annoyed that I was not quick enough to stop him. Later on I casually stated that I had had a glass of ale at Grosmont. He commented severely on my intemperance and moral depravity. Curious enough my naturalness is taken advantage of by some people who make impudent remarks. But I shall always be natural so I must suffer fools gladly.

Frank Elgee

Outside Cranswick Hall, near Great Driffield

THREE TO A HORSE

The great object in travelling then was not to get about the country, but to get to a market – otherwise people usually stayed at home, because travelling was dangerous. It was considered rash to go to London without first making your will, and ungracious to go a hundred miles away without having a farewell feast for all your neighbours, and they all gathered to 'see you off.'

Practically all travel was on horseback, but it was quite common for two or even three to ride one horse. A man on a good horse, overtaking an acquaintance walking, would ask him to get up behind. Sometimes, two men on going the same journey, would share a horse by 'riding and tying.' One would ride a mile, tie the horse to a gate, and walk on, whilst his companion, who had started on foot, would walk up, mount the horse in his turn, and so on, riding and walking a mile each the whole day long.

C.J.F. Atkinson

PRIVILEGES OF FIRST-CLASS TRAVEL

A rather good story is told of a stranger journeying to a far distant dale in Yorkshire. On arrival at the railway terminus he proceeded to engage a seat in a conveyance plying to his destination. Asked if he required a first-, second-, or third-class ticket, he took a first-class, though not a little mystified by the request. This mystification became annoyance when at the appointed time all crowded into the conveyance without any distinction of class. He naturally thought he had been 'had.' However, after a five-mile run on the level, the driver pulled up at the foot of a tremendously long steep hill. 'First-class passengers,' he directed, 'sit still, second-class passengers get out and walk, third-class passengers shove up behind.'

R.W.S. Bishop

A rest from road-mending at Aislaby

Beach transport at Filey

Unknown cyclist near Market Weighton

THE INCALCULABLE BOON OF STEAM ROLLERS

The first steam-roller which came to the moorlands caused much excitement and wonder among the moormen. Crowds gathered to watch it at work. One big fellow became so excited that he had a bad fit and was carried to a moorland inn, where he died six weeks afterwards. The steam-roller was condemned of course at first as a useless expense, but what an incalculable boon and comfort it was. Moorland roads in hot summer weather become exceptionally dry, and before the day of the roller loose stones were everywhere. Even behind the safest of horses there was always anxiety.

R.W.S. Bishop

A CYCLIST IN NEED OF A BEAM AND PULLEYS

I had not gone far before the undulating ridge broke off sharply and let me down into the valley by a steep descent, followed by a sharper rise. The road became decidedly difficult; the surface was by no means dry, and suddenly out of the still sky there swept a blast of chilly wind, there was a roll of thunder far down on the horizon, the sky darkened in a few minutes to an inky blackness, and almost without notice such a storm of rain hissed down upon the sodden earth as might send the stoutest of mankind pelting to the nearest shelter. For me there was no shelter on that accursed road. There would be some loss of dignity in recounting the state to which I was reduced, when the tyranny of that tempest was overpast, and the deluge subsided to a steady drizzle. Nor would it be fitting to relate in what temper I climbed the hills that lay before me, nor with what fond hope I looked out vainly for an inn. At length I saw a welcome signpost which informed me that I was no more than a mile and a half from Levisham station, and I shot off like a homing pigeon on the shocking byway to which the broken finger-board directed me. It led me through a

Bedale Cycling Club, 1897

meagre, miserable village, where the only sign of life proceeded from a tinkling blacksmith's shop. The man at work was civil but amused. He smiled largely as he stood in his doorway answering my questions. Yes, the station was straight on; the road was easy to find, a bit hilly to be sure. I cut him rather short and plodded on. In one mile, I argued, the hills could not be intolerable.

Alas! I did not know. My knowledge of the land of Cleveland is wider now. The road began to drop. It coiled a little so that I could not see its full iniquity, but trudged on gamely thinking I was near the bottom. I met a postman. He laughed and turned to watch me. I knew why presently, for I was on the brow of what could only by the grossest flattery be called a ravine. It was an abyss, and the road ran straight down by a gradient which was even as the gradient of a teacup. Down below me, in the very bowels of the earth, was a pretty valley, winding among the steep shags of gorse and

ling that dropped precipitously to it on every side. I could hear the gushing of a mill leat swollen by the rains, and a small grey church stood midway in the narrow meadow which occupied the valley bottom. The chilly wind blew up the odours of damp woodland, and through the fresh shoots of the springing bracken I could see the quick brown ears of rabbits glancing on the further slope. Higher up the grey rock cropped out, and from one of the grassy shelves, a sheep, entangled in some mass of thorns, filled the whole valley with its piteous bleating. I could have found it in my heart to lament as noisily as he, and in good truth I hold that he who takes a cycle by that road needs no less assistance than a beam and pulleys. I looked back. The postman was still watching me, and I could hear his odious chuckles as he turned to climb the hill.

Arthur H. Norway

Statue of the Black Prince, City Square, Leeds

SHEFFIELD: THE SUNNIEST PLACE IN ENGLAND

Sheffield has a world-wide reputation for its cutlery and for its other productions in brass, iron, and steel, for the manufacture of which pure water of a particular variety was essential. The town was well provided in that respect, for no less than five rivers flowed towards Sheffield from the Pennine range above. From the finest steel all sorts of things were made, ranging from the smallest needle or steel pen up to the largest-sized gun or armour-plate. It would no doubt have interested us greatly to look through one of the works, but such as we passed were labelled 'No admittance except on business,' which we interpreted to mean that no strangers were allowed to enter, lest they might carry away with them the secrets of the business, so we walked slowly onward in the hope of reaching, before nightfall, our next great object of interest, 'The Great Cavern and Castle of Peveril of the Peak.' Passing along the Ecclesall Road, we saw, in nicely wooded enclosures, many of the houses of manufacturers and merchants, who, like ourselves in after life, left their men to sleep in the smoke while they themselves went to breathe the purer air above, for Ecclesall was at a fair elevation above the town. But one gentleman whom we saw assured us that, in spite of the heavy clouds of smoke we had seen, the town was very healthy, and there was more sunshine at Sheffield than in any other town in England.

R.N. and J.N.

LEEDS: A GREAT BLACK CITY

The great black city of Leeds has a nucleus consisting of several fine streets possessing numbers of modern buildings, making an imposing effect worthy of the fifth English city and the commercial capital of Yorkshire. New public buildings, banks, shops, or whatever they may be, however white they commence their existence, in a very short time are toned down to the uniform sable tones of the whole city. Clock-faces stand out with painful whiteness against the sooty stonework of towers and gables, and the only colour to be seen is restricted to the shop-windows. Architects should remember the atmosphere of Leeds, and use coloured glazed bricks and porcelain extensively, so that whole buildings could every year be washed down from the roofs to the ground, and cheer the citizens of the great town with their cleanliness and colour. In City Square, just outside the stations of the Midland, Great Northern, and other railways, and therefore where people get their first impression of Leeds, stands a fine statue of the Black Prince mounted on a noble charger. It seems curiously appropriate that the one member of the royal line of England with such a distinction should have been chosen for a prominent statue in the chief of the black cities of England, especially when we know that Edward III's son was, according to tradition, instrumental in introducing the weaving industry from Flanders into Yorkshire, where it has flourished increasingly ever since. Edward III has been called 'the father of English industry,' and if this is a justifiable distinction both he and his son are in a measure responsible for the blackness as well as the riches their foresight has produced.

Gordon Home

RUNNING THE IRON ROAD TO HAWES

Some time ago now it was no uncommon thing to hear in Hawes (from persons who had at least fifty summers and who were in favour of travelling with the old stage coach and paying 1s carriage on a letter) to say that it was a pity to see green fields cut up for a railway, and to argue with all the potinency of their natures that there is nothing like an old–fashioned warp after all. Since the introduction of railways into our neighbourhood, we have had the advantage never possessed by former generations. Now we have London newspapers, if we choose, delivered on the same day of issue. Now we have two deliveries of letters per day, viz at 9.30am and 6pm, an advantage which is highly appreciated by the inhabitants of Hawes. For the second delivery we are greatly, if not altogether indebted to our able postmaster, Mr E. Blythe, whose efforts to serve his fellow townsmen are untiring and unceasing. Now we have our merchandises brought to our doors at considerably less cost, and with half

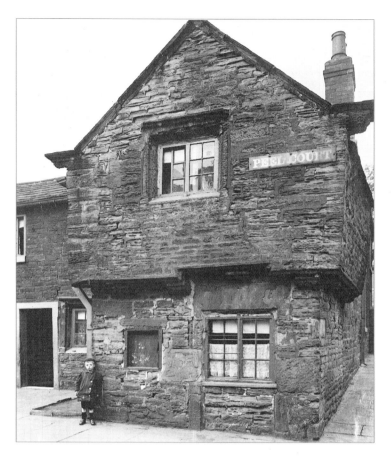

Peel Court, Leeds

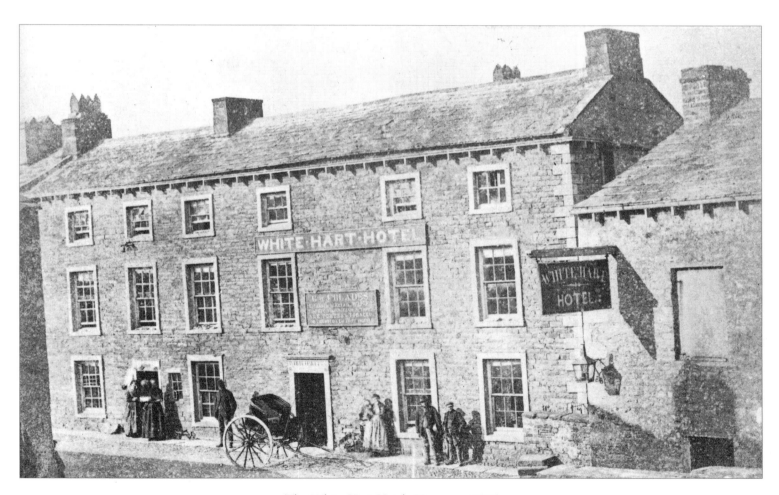

The White Hart Hotel, Hawes, c. 1878

An early motorist pauses near the summit of Buttertubs Pass

the delay, and what is prized by all, both rich and poor, we have coals at the station yard, at from 6½*d* per cwt, good household coals. Who, we ask, would like to return to the old fashioned way of carting them (coals) 16 miles or more? Then, again, what a saving is effected by private individuals wishing to visit their friends living in any of the large towns, or tradespeople who have periodically to visit the markets at Manchester, Liverpool or London; who had to suffer the inclemency of the weather for 16 or 17 miles over wild moors and unsheltered roads, paying 16*s* or 21*s* for such a ride as the old fashioned ways afforded. Now they can travel, as it is needless to say, for infinitely less money and with incomparable comfort. Such are the advantages we in Hawes are deriving from railway connections; who would like to go back to the old times; or who would be grieved at running the iron road through the beautiful green fields of Wensleydale?

Craven Herald and Pioneer, *12 October 1878*

BUTTERTUBS PASS: THE WILDEST SPOT IN ENGLAND

This pass, which earns that title more on account of its steepness than its height, is the ancient road between Swaledale and Wensleydale, and only a very little while ago it was the wildest spot in one of the remotest byways of England. A daring wanderer or two has left a chronicle behind to tell of his great explorations in the Yorkshire Dales, but for years together, pedlars, and farmers, and people belonging as much to this wild region as the stones and heather, were the only travellers upon this lonely path. And, as they lived by dairy produce, it was natural enough to give the name of Buttertubs to the circular chasms in the limestone just below the summit. They are dark, cavernous pits, walled round with splintered limestone which takes many fantastic shapes, and there is no wonder that many tales have been told about strange crimes committed on the Buttertubs Pass.

No one with an imagination, standing there towards the end of a grey day, could fail to picture other travellers in the past who must have been benighted in that lonely spot – the very atmosphere demands a fierce shepherd, driven by envy and hunger, and a hawker with his valuable pack, or a farmer with the payment for wool and cheeses in his pocket.

There must be many such tales unwritten and only lingering on in the minds of some old men and women who will never tell, but a sufficient number have been preserved to make the Buttertubs Pass an eerie place unless you go over it at high noon in the sunshine, though Shummer Fell is only 2000 feet, and Lovely Seat, which faces it, is still lower.

It is a steep and tiresome road, and every green ridge climbed reveals another to be surmounted after, but at last the summit is reached, and there spreads before the eye a wonderful panorama of this vast hill-country. One shadowy hilltop rises behind the other, and along the wide, open valleys shine the emerald pastures of Wensleydale. The first real knowledge comes home to you, then, of the jewelled colouring which is refreshing your jaded sight as the air is stimulating your tired brain.

For that is one great charm of these sister dales of Wensleydale and Swaledale – the clear blue of the flowers, the strong, pure green of the trees and fields, the golden water.

J.E. Buckrose

Advertising postcard issued by Simpson's Car Sales, York, 1904

GHASTLY SIGNS OF THE MODERN TEMPER

I have been driving by the old road from Coniston here through Kirkby Lonsdale, and have seen more ghastly signs of modern temper than I yet had believed possible.

The valley of the Lune at Kirkby is one of the loveliest scenes in England – therefore in the world. Whatever moorland, hill and sweet view and English forest foliage can be seen at their best is gathered there; and chiefly seen from the steep bank which falls to the stream side from the upper part of the town itself. There, a path leads from the churchyard out of which Turner made his drawing of the valley, along the brow of the woodland bank, to open downs beyond; a little bye footpath on the right descending steeply through the woods to a spring among the rocks of the shore. I do not know in all my own country, still less in France or Italy, a place more naturally divine, or a more priceless possession of true 'Holy Land'.

Well, the population of Kirkby cannot, it appears, in consequence of their recent civilisation, any more walk, on summer afternoons, along the brows of this bank, without a fence. I first fancied this was because they were usually unable to take care of themselves at that period of the day; but saw presently I must be mistaken in that conjecture, because the fence they have put up requires far more sober minds for safe dealing with than ever the bank did; being of thin, strong, and finely sharpened skewers, on which if a drunken man rolled heavily, he would assuredly be impaled at the armpit. They have carried this lovely decoration down on both sides of the woodpath to the spring, with warning notices on ticket – 'This path leads only to the ladies' well – all trespassers will be prosecuted' and the iron rails leave so narrow footing that I myself scarcely ventured to go down – the morning being frosty, and the path slippery – lest I should fall on the spikes. The wall at the bottom was choked up and defaced with iron all round so as to look like the 'pound' of old days for strayed cattle: they had been felling the trees too; and the old wood had protested against the

fence in its own way, with its last root and branch – for the falling trunks had crashed through the iron gating in all directions, and left it in already rusty and unseemly rags, like the last refuse of a railroad accident, beaten down among dead leaves.

The same morning I had to water my horse at the little village of Clapham, between Kirkby and Settle. There is another exquisite rocky brook there; and an old bridge over it. I went down to the brook-side to see the old bridge; and found myself instantly, of course, stopped by a dunghill, and that of the vilest human sort; while, just on the other side of the road, not twenty yards off, were the new schools, with their orthodox Gothic belfry – all spick and span – and the children playing fashionably at hoop, round them, in a narrow paved yard – like debtor children in the Fleet, in imitation of the manners and customs of the West End. High over all, the Squire's house, resplendent on the hill-side, within sight of belfry and brook.

I got on here, to Bolton Bridge, the same day; and walked to the Abbey in the evening, to look again at Turner's subject at the Wharfe shore. If there is one spot in England where human creatures pass or live, which one would expect to find, in *spite* of their foul existence, still clean, it is Bolton Park. But to my final and utter amazement, I had not taken two steps by the waterside at the loveliest bend in the river below the stepping stones, before I found myself again among the broken crockery, cinders, cockle-shells and tinkers' refuse; – a large old gridiron forming the principal point of effect and interest among the pebbles. The filth must be regularly carried past the Abbey, and across the Park, to the place.

John Ruskin

ENVOI

'ONE LOVELY DAY IN LATE SUMMER . . . '

O ne lovely day in late Summer when the bracken on our hills was just beginning to go rusty, and the swallows were starting to muster, the strains of marching music and the tramp of marching men, came down the road; men in khaki with rifles at the slope, smart and proud, some with faces set and grim, some devil-may-care. A sharp command, a stamping halt, and a brief release while wives and children, sweethearts and friends, kissed, shook hands, and said Goodbye! The band struck up:

> Farewell, farewell – my own true home,
> I cannot bear to leave you . . .
> I go where duty calls me . . .

and tears trickled and flowed, and people waved and shouted, and the train moved off with khaki filling every door and window, and Bob Storey's fog signals along the line popped in succession as the engine pulled away and 'D' Coy. of the 4th Yorks. Territorial Battalion went off to war on that lovely late Summer day in 1914.

Maurice E. Wilson

Yeomanry camp at Helmsley, 1909

The Scots Greys leave Kirkbymoorside, 25 July 1912

PHOTOGRAPHIC CREDITS AND TEXT SOURCES

ILLUSTRATIONS

The photographs in this book are reproduced courtesy of the following, with the illustrations listed by page number. The author's thanks are due to:

Basil Allen for 98 (upper picture), 109 (lower picture)

Bradford Libraries for 4, 70 (lower picture), 90

Huddersfield Libraries for the front endpaper, iv, 10 (upper picture), 69

Ken Jackson of Memory Lane, Hull, for i, ii, iii, v, vi, 10 (lower picture), 14, 20 (lower picture), 24 (upper picture), 29, 36 (right-hand picture), 53, 63, 67, 74, 75, 76, 78, 96, 101 (lower picture)

Kingston upon Hull Libraries for 95

Leeds Libraries for 15, 33, 55 (lower picture), 68, 109 (upper picture)

Marks & Spencer for 21

Betty Matthews of Hampsthwaite for 6 (left-hand picture), 19, 23, 43 (lower picture), 87 (lower picture)

North Yorkshire County Records Office, Northallerton, for 3, 52 (lower picture), 56, 107

Mrs J. Pickup of Pickering for 1, 2 (lower picture), 5 (lower picture), 7, 9, 17, 20, 24 (lower picture), 25, 26, 42, 44 (both pictures), 46, 47, 48 (left-hand picture), 50 (upper picture), 52 (upper picture), 54, 57, 58 (upper picture), 59, 62, 65, 66, 70 (upper picture), 79 (lower picture), 84 (lower picture), 89 (upper picture), 90 (lower picture), 92, 93, 99, 102 (right-hand picture), 106 (all pictures), 112 (both pictures)

The Sutcliffe Gallery, Whitby, for 16, 34, 40 (lower picture), 43, 45, 72, 103, back endpaper

Swaledale Folk Museum, Reeth, for 58 (lower picture), 83

Ray Wilkinson for 61 (lower picture)

Remaining photographs are from the author's collection.

TEXT

The page numbers given below relate to pages in this book and not the page numbers of the source books.

The main sources for descriptive text are: C.J.F. Atkinson, *Recollections from a Yorkshire Dale*, pp. 8, 9, 11, 37, 38, 42–4, 46, 47, 88, 90, 91, 94, 95, 105, 106. Lady Bell, *At The Works*, 25, 37, 38, 71, 72. R.W.S. Bishop, *My Moorland Patients*, 5, 50, 51, 82, 83, 105. Richard Blakeborough, *Yorkshire: Wit, Character, Folklore & Customs*, 6, 7, 18, 19, 31, 32, 35, 36. Christabel Burniston, *Life in a Liberty Bodice*, 19, 20, 21, 91, 92. Capt. F. Chapman, *Reminiscences of the Wensleydale Hounds, 1775–1907*, 11, 62, 63, 64, 65. J. Fairfax-Blakeborough, *Yorkshire: Village Life, Humour and Characters*, 6, 32, 39, 42, 45, 47–50, 61, 62, 83, 84. Gordon Home, *Yorkshire*, 33, 35, 95, 99, 100, 108, 109; *Yorkshire Dales & Fells*, 36. Thomas and Katherine McQuaid, *About Yorkshire*, 5, 68, 69, 88, 102.

Other sources are: William E. Anderton, *Reminiscences of Yorkshire Life and Humour*, 9, 70, 71, 102. William Linton Andrews, *Yorkshire Folk*, 7. Canon J.C. Atkinson, *Forty Years in a Moorland Parish*, 39. Edmund Bogg, *The Old Kingdom of Elmet*, 32, 92–4; *Wild Borderland of Richmondshire*, 13, 57, 59; *Higher Wharfedale*, 31, 56; *1000 Miles in Wharfedale*, 60, 61. Horace B. Browne, *Story of the East Riding of Yorkshire*, 77. J.E. Buckrose, *Rambles in the North Yorkshire Dales*, 110, 111. Daisy Burton, *Remembering*, 25. Fred Cobley, *On Foot Through Wharfedale*, 60. Frank Elgee, *A Man of the Moors*, 103, 104. Brenda H. English, *Five Generations of a Whitby Medical Family*, 88. Harry Fletcher, *A Life on the Humber*, 78–81. Joseph Ford, *Some Reminiscences and Folklore of Danby Parish and District*, 29, 30, 33, 57. Miss M.W.E. Fowler, *Memorials of Old Yorkshire*, 18, 30, 36, 37. Samuel Gordon, *Watering Places of Cleveland*, 103. George Hardcastle, *Wanderings in Wensleydale*, 98. Michael Heavisides, *Rambles in Cleveland*, 48, 59, 99. *Huddersfield College Magazine*, Autumn 1891, 65, 66. *Huddersfield Year Book*, 1897, 54. Storm Jameson, *Journey to the North*, vol 1, 23, 25. James Russell Lowell, *Letters*, 103. C.J. Maltby, *Yorkshire for Me*, 48, 54, 56. *Middlesbrough Daily Exchange*, 26, 73, 74. Revd M.C.F. Morris, *Yorkshire Folk Talk*, 74, 75. R.N and J.N., *From John O'Groats to Lands End*, 100, 101, 108. Arthur H. Norway, *Highways and Byways in Yorkshire*, 14, 15, 106, 107. Herbert Read, *The Innocent Eye*, 23. B. Seebohm Rowntree, *Poverty*, 85, 86. Harry J. Scott, *Further Up the Dale*, 42. H.B. Sellers, *Memoranda from a Notebook on the Yorkshire Penny Bank*, 6. Harry Speight, *Romantic Richmondshire*, 98, 99. Halliwell Sutcliffe, *By Moor and Fell*, 12, 13. Ben Turner, *About Myself*, 68, 69, 70, 84, 85. *Whitby Gazette*, 72, 73. *Whitby Observer*, 57. Maurice E. Wilson, *The Story of Eston*, 112. *Yorkshire Men of Mark*, 91.

INDEX